THE QUIET
REVOLUTION

THE QUIET REVOLUTION

Jay F. Hein

Waterfall
PRESS

Published by Waterfall Press

www.apub.com

ISBN 13: 9781477819586
ISBN 10: 1477819584

Library of Congress Control Number: 2013954702

Printed in the United States of America
First printing—October 2013

To my parents for teaching me to love others.
To my wife Mary Jo and children Ali, T.J., and
Ryan for loving me so well.

TABLE OF CONTENTS

FOREWORD

I have spent the better part of three decades serving in the United States Congress. This was never my plan. I loved the law but thought I would practice it as a lawyer rather than create it as a lawmaker. Then I met Chuck Colson.

With a law degree from Indiana University and a good job working for a life insurance company in Fort Wayne, I found myself captivated by a former lawyer who spoke to our city's prayer breakfast in April 1976. Colson told us his story, which went from loving the law to breaking it and subsequently led to his fall from Richard Nixon's aide in the White House to a resident of Maxwell Prison in Alabama.

Newly released from prison and author of a just-released book called *Born Again*, Colson's message of restorative justice touched me deeply. He challenged me to give up the control I enjoyed in my comfortable life and give over that control to God, who may have a different plan for my life.

Thirty-six years after meeting Chuck at that Fort Wayne prayer breakfast, I eulogized my friend from the floor of the United States Senate. His life proved that faith in God could transform not only his own heart but those of the countless prisoners whom he loved over the decades.

His ministry proved that the same faith could inform a justice that did not ignore wrongs but did not see punishment as the goal.

Restoration was the goal, along with prevention and community well-being.

These ideas have shaped my views in Congress. Along with another friend, William J. Bennett, I crafted the Project for American Renewal in 1994. We studied the rising crises of teenage pregnancy, random violence, and other social ills and rejected the conventional wisdom that these things were simply by-products of economic inequality. We felt that a breakdown in personal responsibility and values was the real culprit.

We also understood that the only remedies to these ills were stronger families, churches, neighborhoods, and voluntary associations. These institutions are sometimes called civil society and they are the only known immune system to combat cultural disease. These are the only groups who can tend to an individual's heart, yet whose collective actions benefit millions.

When private charities are strong, they comprise a force that lifts people and communities. When they are weak, no amount of police or public spending can provide a substitute. As a policy maker, I tried to square this circle. In other words, what could I do in government to support non-government groups?

For starters, government needs to do no harm. Yet that has been the case for the second half of the last century. Fathers have been replaced by welfare checks, private charities displaced by government spending, religious volunteers dismissed as "amateurs," and whole neighborhoods demolished in slum-clearance projects. The power to replace an institution is the power to destroy it.

The 1996 welfare reform law started the process of restoring the place of religious charities in the public square, and President Bush's effort to level the playing field completed it. Today's policy makers need to hold this ground in order to re-limit government, leaving enough social space for civil society to resume its role.

Our tax code is another way for government to help the helpers. Since conservative social reengineering is as futile as the liberal version, there cannot be a government plan to rebuild civil society. But incentivizing private giving is a very effective way to take the side of charities carrying their neighbors' burdens with massive spirit but meager resources.

I had the experience of seeing how religious charities not only feed the body but touch the soul. They are dramatically effective, while the programs I re-authorized year after year in Congress did not even bother to keep track of their dismal results. One of my favorite programs was the Gospel Mission in Washington, D.C. It has a twelve-month drug rehabilitation rate of 66 percent, while a once-heralded government program just three blocks away rehabilitates less than 10 percent of those it serves. Yet the government program spends many times more per person.

I was moved by one addict who came to the shelter after failing in several government programs who said, "Those programs generally take addictions from you, but they don't place anything within you. I needed a spiritual lifting. People like those at the mission are like God walking into your life. Not only am I drug-free, but more than that, I can be a person again."

Following Marvin Olasky's charge to "defund" government and "refund" private charities, Bill Bennett and I made tax incentives central to our Project for American Renewal. Every dollar spent by families, community groups, and faith-based charities is more efficient and compassionate than any dollar spent by the federal government. Our objective was to promote a new ethic of giving in America.

When individuals make contributions to effective charities, it is a form of involvement beyond writing a check to the federal government. It encourages a new definition of citizenship—one in which men and women examine and support the programs in their own communities that serve the poor. And with their money, so too should follow their time and talent.

I learned this approach by doing. During my life in Fort Wayne before politics, I was privileged to meet C.J. Bundy in 1972 when he allowed me to be his Big Brother. C.J. was struggling in elementary school at the time, but he put in the work to become a good student and eventually a professional and family man. He gave me the great honor of being best man in his wedding.

When I left the U.S. Senate in 1998 to honor my term-limit pledge, I continued my public service as national board president for Big Brothers Big Sisters. With my wife, Marsha, I also created the Foundation for American Renewal to advocate for effective compassion and to provide funding for faith-based solutions to poverty.

These streams flowed together when the foundation provided a grant to Big Brothers Big Sisters in 1999 to support their new initiative to provide mentoring for children of prisoners. Those children are seven times more likely to follow their mom or dad's life of crime unless the pattern is broken by other caring adults.

It was with great satisfaction that I watched President Bush's 2003 State of the Union address announcing that he would launch his own "Mentoring Children of Prisoners" initiative. Working largely with churches, the Bush administration reached its goal of 100,000 mentors for these children by the end of 2008.

Jay F. Hein had a unique vantage point in the president's collaboration with Big Brothers Big Sisters as well as in so many other inspiring stories that you'll read in this terrific book. I have enjoyed being Jay's partner in advancing faith-based social enterprise since I recruited him to direct the Foundation for American Renewal while I served as U.S. Ambassador to Germany during

President Bush's first term. Upon my return to the States, President Bush invited Jay to serve as White House faith-based director. In both of these roles, no one has formed a clearer line of sight to winning the war on poverty, armed with spiritual vitality, tough love, and true, effective compassion.

I returned to the U.S. Senate in 2010 to fight for fiscal discipline, yet my heart remains with the Foundation for American Renewal and our faith-based and community partners. I am grateful to Jay for writing this book and for serving the servants in communities across America. You will be inspired and challenged by this book, and I hope you'll be motivated to put your faith in action after you read it.

The Honorable Daniel R. Coats
United States Senator

INTRODUCTION

The twenty-first century began with a rise of terrorism and a global economic crisis. These unwelcome forces have dominated headlines, sparked protests, and influenced elections for a decade. However, largely unnoticed during this same time has been a dramatic rise in generosity and a steep decline in global poverty. This quiet revolution is fueled by compassion, faith-inspired service, and strategic social investments in place of well-intended but often failed aid.

Citizens have always been at the center of solving our nation's most pressing human needs. The French political philosopher Alexis de Toqueville observed that when tragedy befalls an American citizen, the purse strings of a thousand strangers open up.[1] That has never been more true than in the first decade of the twenty-first century.

Between the years 2000 and 2010, the number of nonprofits in America grew by nearly 25 percent to total 1.6 million. These organizations create one in ten jobs in the American economy and hold a combined asset base of $2.7 trillion. If America's nonprofit

---

[1] "When an American asks for the co-operation of his fellow-citizens it is seldom refused, and I have often seen it afforded spontaneously and with great goodwill. If an accident happens on the highway, everybody hastens to help the sufferer; if some great and sudden calamity befalls a family, the purses of a thousand strangers are at once willingly opened, and small but numerous donations pour in to relieve their distress." Alexis de Toqueville, *Democracy in America Volume 2* (Indianapolis: The Liberty Fund, 2012), 1005.

sector were a national economy, it would rank in size larger than France's economy.

Fueling all this activity is the breathtaking growth of philanthropy. Just fifteen years ago, charitable giving hovered around $150 billion. During the Bush administration, philanthropy topped $300 billion for the first time in history. Three in four Americans give to charity, and thousands of philanthropic foundations are created each year. Boston College reports that the over $40 trillion will transfer from one generation to another over the next fifty years.[2] Thanks to the rise of new strategies such as donor-advised funds, as well as tax advantages to giving, much of this intergenerational transfer of wealth will result in increased philanthropy.

Peter Drucker called such compassion America's greatest export. Over the past ten years, it has contributed to one of the greatest humanitarian success stories of all time. In 1999–2000, more Africans died from AIDS than in all the previous wars on the continent. It was the largest health pandemic on the planet and 24 million Africans faced a death sentence. Within a decade, 8 million AIDS patients have received lifesaving medicine, malaria deaths have been cut by 75 percent, and death rates for children age five years or under have been reduced by 2.65 million per year. African parents used to wait several months after giving birth to name their baby for fear it wouldn't survive. Now that over 7,000 children's lives are being saved each day, Africans have a newfound hope.[3]

Over the same time period in the United States, faith-based and community organizations contributed to impressive gains in the fight against criminal recidivism, drug addiction, school dropout rates,

---

[2] John J. Havens and Paul G. Schervish, "Millionaires and the Millennium: New Estimates of the Forthcoming Wealth Transfer and the Prospects for a Golden Age of Philanthropy," Social Welfare Research Institute (1999).

[3] Bono, "Eradicating Extreme Poverty Doesn't Have to Be a Dream," TED Talk (2013).

and other key social issues. This book tells those stories. The principal character is an American president who created a faith-based initiative to drive his compassion agenda, achieving dramatic gains in human well-being. Most of the pages also belong to the hometown heroes who put their faith into action quietly and powerfully to vanquish the enemies of disease, crime, poverty, and injustice.

People, not bureaucracies, solve problems. America's extravagant generosity—both in manpower and money—stands at tens of millions of volunteers and hundreds of billions of dollars aimed toward our neighbors in need each year. The nonprofit sector is the fastest growing segment of American economy, yet we continue to refer to it by what it is not. Sure, it doesn't deliver profits for privately held interests, but it does produce over a trillion dollars in revenue each year (totaling 5.5 percent of the nation's entire GDP) invested in improved lives and communities. In other words, volunteers are "public profits."

From the White House, George W. Bush sought to harness these armies of compassion for even greater good. This was a delicate work of reforming government to welcome new partners while not taking away the unique qualities of private voluntary organizations. It also widened the public square to faith-based groups without imposing faith on others. Finally, it brought all Americans together by a call to service that unites us in a common endeavor.

Taken together, the Bush compassion agenda contributed mightily to the quiet revolution that has achieved so much for so many. This book attempts to explain this success by examining the following major Bush administration themes:

1) *A presidential call to service* that continues a legacy begun by George Washington and renewed by President Bush, who called on Americans to be the first responders to human need.

This call was made more urgent following 9/11 when we were not called to fight on the war front or ration goods at home. Rather, President Bush asked us to serve our nation by serving our communities. Effective compassion is a personal business conducted in relationships, not public policy.

2) *Declaring human needs unacceptable.* Through effective use of the White House bully pulpit, the faith-based initiative took dead aim at the most urgent struggles being faced today. When nearly half of urban school kids don't graduate from high school and almost 30 million adults and children are held captive in modern-day slavery,[4] the only response is "Unacceptable!" Declaring an attack on need, the compassion agenda matched an unflinching view of human struggle with portraits of nonprofits bringing hope, healing, and strategies to further their success.

3) *The power of faith to transform lives and revitalize communities.* From Moses leading the Israelites out of captivity to Rev. Martin Luther King, Jr., leading America to a more perfect union, faith has inspired the pursuit of justice. Faith also motivates outrageous generosity—in giving of both oneself and one's resources. Harvard sociologist Robert Putnam claims that religion is the number one predictor of giving and serving in America.[5]

4) *Government policies focused on results and incentivizing private enterprise.* When government is buying social services, the emphasis should be on desired outcomes and

---

[4] Christopher Swanson, "Cities in Crisis 2009: Closing the Graduation Gap" (Bethseda: Editorial Projects in Education, 2009).

[5] Robert Putnam, *Amazing Grace: How Religion Divides and Unites Us* (New York: Simon & Schuster, 2010).

accountability. Yet government spending should never crowd out private enterprise, which is larger and more sustainable in building better societies. Entrepreneurship and social investments are twenty-first century tools necessary to enjoy a brighter future.

Citizens, Not Spectators

Then-Governor Bush explained his compassion agenda vision for the first time in a July 1999 speech called "The Duty of Hope." Addressing a racially diverse crowd at Indianapolis' Metro Church, he said, "Our country must be prosperous. But prosperity must have a purpose. The purpose of prosperity is to make sure the American dream touches every willing heart. The purpose of prosperity is to leave no one out—to leave no one behind."[6]

He continued by saying, "When a life is broken, it can only be rebuilt by another caring, concerned human being. Someone whose actions say, 'I love you, I believe in you, I'm in your corner.'" It was in this context that he established the framework for his faith-based initiative. Bush signaled his intent to rally America's armies of compassion through charitable giving incentives and then said, "In every instance where my administration sees a responsibility to help people, we will look first to faith-based organizations, charities, and community groups that have shown their ability to save and change lives."

Following 9/11, volunteerism reversed its forty-year decline with a patriotic boost, and the trend of skilled volunteerism took flight. President Kennedy's inaugural address challenge ("Ask not what your country can do for you but what you can do for your

---

[6] http://blog.chron.com/txpotomac/2010/07/today-in-texas-history-gw-bush-delivers-first-presidential-campaign-speech.

country") inspired many to join the Peace Corps and other noble public service offices. However, the Baby Boom generation volunteered their time much less than their World War II generation parents who followed their military tours of duty with active community service.

Calling himself a compassionate conservative, Bush knew that his call to service was not standard GOP-primary rhetoric, but neither was it a new message crafted for the campaign. It was personal for him. It is widely known that as a forty-year-old businessman struggling with success and alcohol, Bush had a conversion experience influenced by family mentor Billy Graham. Faith was the defining characteristic that turned his life around and made possible his pursuit of public office, a healthy family, and a meaningful life. He knew that type of transformation worked across socioeconomic lines, and he also knew it was impossible for government to deliver. This type of change could only work on a human scale.

Once in office, President Bush sought to match the power of government with the personal touch and transformative effect of small, neighborhood-based organizations. He created the Office of Faith-Based and Community Initiatives as the vehicle to carry the compassion agenda forward. Much of this book illustrates how the faith-based initiative targeted dozens of the nation's worst human struggles. I had the privilege of leading the White House Office of Faith Based and Community Initiatives under President Bush, and I am eager to share the *real* story here, one which very few know.

What the Faith-Based Initiative Was Really About

First of all, let me describe what this initiative was *not*.

It was *not* about legislation on Capitol Hill.
It was *not* about mixing politics and religion.

It was *not* about giving money to favored churches or charities.

It was *not* about picking one religion or another or even religion over non-religion.

It was *not* about what happens in Washington, D.C.

The faith-based initiative *was* about citizens solving problems in their communities and government learning how to support them effectively in those efforts. It was about championing the unsung work of ordinary volunteers, of faith and goodwill, who rolled up their sleeves and took personal responsibility for helping their neighbors in need. It was about recognizing that the First Amendment does not prohibit faith in the public square nor the sensible partnership of public agencies with private ones that share their goals to see the homeless housed, the hungry fed, the lonely kids mentored, the vulnerable protected, the sick brought succor, the unemployed put to work, and the prisoners rehabilitated.

It *was* about public and private generosity. It was about the biggest investments by any Administration in humanitarian aid to save lives in Africa and restore the lives of prisoners and drug addicts here at home. It was about re-envisioning such aid to distribute it through new channels, with far higher degrees of accountability and expectations for real results. It was about recognizing that private aid matters far more than public, and that investment trumps aid all together.

It was mainly about activities *outside* Washington's power corridors—reforms and new initiatives among state and local governments that are routinely dismissed by political and media elites but actually affect the day-to-day lives of the majority of Americans. Yes, it was a White House initiative, but what the chattering classes could never seem to grasp was that its progress had to be measured in real changes in people's lives "back home" rather than in "who's up and who's down" in Washington. The national media stubbornly tried to find the faith-based initiative's storyline in congressional legislation and other federal action, but the real work was being done on the civic frontlines.

A Map of This Book

When George W. Bush took office, our nation still practiced religious discrimination as the last acceptable prejudice. As he left office, the term "faith-based" was used commonly and positively. As President Bush's faith-based director, I met many inner-city pastors who asked me to thank the president on their behalf. Before the faith-based initiative, they were deemed suspect or even considered a negative influence in the public square. Because of the initiative, they are now not only welcomed but often the first ones officials call upon when problems arise. The public value of private religion is now much more clearly understood and appreciated.

It was my great honor to serve a president who believed that government should be limited but also accountable and competent. More so, he shared his father's belief that any definition of a successful life must include service to others and that compassion should be measured in results, not intentions. These themes are woven throughout this book amid faith- and community-based stories of restorative justice, recovery from drug addiction, rescue from domestic violence and human trafficking, recovery from natural disasters, and much more.

Chapter 1 takes readers into the White House to glimpse how President Bush and other presidents called on citizens to serve their nation by serving their communities. The faith-based initiative was about solving problems, and we'll look at the initiative's success in addressing three big ones: effective response to natural disasters, the scourge of drug addiction, and the school dropout crisis.

Chapter 2 takes a deep dive into the multiple dimensions of the phrase "the faith factor." Just what is it that makes faith special? Why does faith matter in terms of the effective delivery of social services, progress in peacemaking, and the seemingly intractable challenges of healing broken lives and communities?

Chapter 3 reviews what the faith-based initiative accomplished in providing restorative justice and help for three highly vulnerable populations: ex-offenders who need to successfully reintegrate into society; children of prisoners who need the deep, personal care of responsible adults to keep them from spiraling into risky behaviors; and women who are victims of human trafficking and domestic violence in need of rescue and healing.

Chapters 4 and 5 take readers to two places that might be unexpected: the states and localities of the nation and abroad to Africa. Because the media insisted on framing the faith-based initiative as an "inside-the-Beltway" story, most Americans are unfamiliar with its truly broad scope. In Chapter 4 we'll look at how states implemented their own versions of the Initiative and the gains they achieved in so doing. Chapter 5 shifts our gaze to Africa, where Bush's compassionate conservatism brought about game-changing results in global health and contributed to a dramatic drop in extreme poverty.

Chapter 6 takes up the topic that got too much attention during the Bush presidency—one that is rife with misconceptions: the appropriate relationship between church and state. I provide a brief education on the history of church/state relations and attempt to explain today's legal landscape. We'll discover the roots of the misunderstandings about what government and the faith community can and can't do together, and we'll trace the arc of church/state jurisprudence to its contemporary position of "equal treatment."

The book closes in Chapter 7 by returning to its central theme: that ultimately the faith-based initiative is less a government policy and more a call to service by citizens, for it is in the innovations and actions of faith-full individuals that the common good will best be advanced. This work happens in cities, not the United States government, and yet we serve our nation when we serve our communities.

To my readers who believe in God, I hope this book inspires you to put your faith in action. To those of you who are skeptical of religion, I hope you will see the public good that results from private faith.

Jay F. Hein
Indianapolis, Indiana

1

UNCLE SAM WANTS YOU

Some problems are simply too big for government to fix. When humans suffer, an impersonal transfer of money or a hot meal deadens the pain, but it does not make it go away. Healing and life change only occurs when one life intersects with another.

George Washington and every president since have called Americans to the duty of citizenship. Many people today think that civic participation is limited to voting in elections, but our nation's leaders have always set the bar much higher. For them, citizenship includes voluntary service to their communities and a willingness to help the hurting.

John F. Kennedy launched the Peace Corps to address global poverty. In a 2:00 a.m. impromptu speech to 5,000 students at the University of Michigan, Kennedy called on America's youth to show the best of our nation to the developing world. Since then, nearly 200,000 of our finest young adults have answered that call in 139 countries. Richard Nixon created the Senior Corps so that older citizens could deploy their time and talent to help others. Jimmy Carter has used his own senior years to wield a hammer and build Habitat for Humanity homes. Ronald Reagan responded to an outbreak of vandalism at our national parks by creating a Take Pride in America volunteerism program aimed at building a national culture of ownership in our public lands. Said Reagan, "All Americans should take pride in their outstanding public lands and historic sites that belong to everyone....We must all work for a renewed awareness that these lands are our lands."[7] Today, 300,000 volunteers serve annually at our nation's parks.[8]

Indeed, all modern U.S. presidents have formed strategies to engage citizens in service to the common good. This ethic is at the heart of our democratic experiment. None captured its meaning better than George H.W. Bush, who often stated that any definition of a successful life must include serving others. When accepting his party's nomination for the presidency in 1988, he celebrated America's service ethic, whereby neighbors have looked first to one another rather than to the state when faced with hardship. He said:

> "[W]e're a nation of community; of thousands and tens of thousands of ethnic, religious, social, business, labor union, neighborhood, regional and other organizations, all of them varied, voluntary and unique...a brilliant diversity spread like the stars, like *a thousand points of light* in a broad and peaceful sky. Does government have a place? Yes. Government is a part of the nation of communities—not the whole, just a part."[9]

While in office, President Bush 41 (as he was later called by his son to distinguish their forty-first and forty-third presidencies in U.S. history) established the Office of National Service and he championed legislation to create the Commission on National and

---

[7] Ronald Reagan, State of the Union Address, 1986.

[8] http://www.takepride.gov/honors2011.cfm.

[9] George H.W. Bush, Address accepting the presidential nomination at the Republican National Convention in New Orleans, August 18, 1988.

Community Service. This new independent federal agency was charged with supporting service-learning and other youth development programs as well as national service-demonstration projects. One of those projects was City Year, which translated Gandhi's admonition to be the change you'd like to see in the world to a program of youth service-rebuilding communities.

On January 20, 1993, President Bush welcomed the Clintons to the White House for coffee before Bill Clinton's inauguration. Following a campaign marked by mutual attacks over economic policy and even personal character, it would have been understandable if they feigned pleasantries. Instead, Bush used the occasion to request that Clinton take care of his "Points of Light."[10]

President Clinton not only kept President Bush's "Points of Light" in place but also made the Bush service commission permanent via 1993 legislation creating the Corporation for National and Community Service. So fond of this work was Bill Clinton that he used his own last day in office to implore his successor to keep it alive. In a poetic gesture of history, Clinton welcomed George W. Bush to coffee on Inauguration Day, and Clinton used the occasion to request that Bush take care of his Corporation for National and Community Service.[11]

The Bush-Clinton-Bush exchange reveals a bipartisan—indeed nonpartisan—rich Oval Office tradition: incubating and sustaining citizen efforts to strengthen the country. Presidents have often deployed citizens as the secret weapon used to combat some of our nation's greatest crises.

---

[10] http://www.pointsoflight.org/blog/2013/04/26/change-notes-presidential-library-opening-prompts-thoughts-legacy-and-service; http://www.dailymail.co.uk/news/article-1368842/Bill-Clinton-George-HW-Bush-reveal-firm-friendship-Points-Light-Institute-gala.html.

[11] "Godfather of National Service Sees Bright Future," Pacific Standard (January 12, 2009) URL: http://www.psmag.com/culture-society/godfather-of-national-service-sees-bright-future-4013/.

Inside the White House

President George W. Bush not only continued the White House emphasis on citizen service, but the scope and size of his actions fundamentally reshaped the way presidents help the helpers. In his very first executive order, Bush established the Office of Faith-Based and Community Initiatives within the White House and used subsequent executive orders to create similar offices at eleven federal agencies.

These faith-based offices were designed to reform government and revitalize society by strengthening grassroots community groups. President Bush cast his vision for the faith-based offices' outreach to communities during this inaugural address: "Our public interest depends on private character, on civic duty and family bonds.... What you do is as important as anything government does. I ask you to seek a common good beyond your comfort ... to serve your nation, beginning with your neighbor. I ask you to be citizens: citizens, not spectators; citizens, not subjects; responsible citizens, building communities of service and a nation of character."[12]

This message about becoming citizens and not mere spectators signaled that the administration's success would be measured not by what was accomplished inside the eighteen acres of the White House complex but whether anything was done to help those who were helping others in need. Core to the president's compassionate conservatism, it was his faith-based offices' job to put government policy in support of local action—rather than the other way around.

It is fair to question just how effectively the White House can connect with local neighborhoods where Americans conduct the business of citizenship and compassion. When asked by the transition team for my input on the faith-based office design, I proposed

---

[12] George W. Bush, Inaugural Address, 2001.

a voluntary network of state offices that would be led by the president. This had the dual value of maximizing the presidential bully pulpit while executing strategies at the state and local level with both public and private leaders. This method had proved successful during welfare reform, and I thought it could be replicated by the faith-based initiative.

The downside of a prominent federal government operation is that it caused the Washington media to place priority on what was happening in Washington instead of the communities. "Inside the Beltway" forces pushed and pulled the faith-based story into debates over church and state, measuring its success by the passage of legislation and the percentage of money spent on this group or that. Lost in this cacophony and national media news cycles was the heart of the faith-based initiative itself: a determined attack on need.

The president wanted to declare each instance of human suffering unacceptable and take steps to defeat these pathologies with innovative faith-based and community strategies. He was inspired by the likes Tony Evans and Bob Woodson who claimed that there wasn't a social problem in America that wasn't being solved in neighborhoods across our country by men and women quietly at work motivated by their faith or goodwill. Again blending his business sense with compassion, Bush favored the emerging field of social entrepreneurship.

> "Neighborhood leaders from across the nation have addressed effectively the most entrenched problems of poverty in many of America's most devastated communities."
>
> —Bob Woodson, social entrepreneur[13]

---

[13] Robert Woodson and Jennifer A. Marshall, "Listening to Local Voices on Poverty," The Heritage Foundation (2012).

The newly formed White House initiative admirably sought tax credits to fuel this movement, and it eliminated much of the government's discrimination against religious charities. However, the game-changer was President Bush himself. Throughout his presidency, Bush gave dozens of speeches all across the country lauding the public service of private actors. He often traveled on Air Force One to visit the unheralded volunteers of inner-city ministries rather than give the more traditional convention center speech to thousands. Bush would pull up in a hardscrabble neighborhood, drape an arm around the pastor's shoulder—much like he did the New York City firefighter after 9/11—and say that when the faithful serve their neighbor in need, they are serving their nation. And he was there to make sure the nation heard from them.

Such presidential advocacy fundamentally changed the culture of faith in America's public square. Countless faith-based leaders testified to the fact that before the Bush faith-based initiative, pastors were deemed off-limits at the decision-making table. They were considered to be dangerous, or they were simply invisible. After hearing the president spend eight years extolling their necessary role in healing communities, faith-based groups now are often among the first to be invited by mayors and civic leaders who seek answers to nagging problems such as crime and injustices like failing schools.

The President's Cabinet

It may seem like a big bureaucratic maneuver to build faith-based offices at eleven federal agencies, but this move ensured that faith-friendly and community-oriented policies were adopted in every human service program across the government. Invited by the president to attend his cabinet meeting in February 2008, I listened to Secretary of State Condoleezza Rice and Defense Secretary Robert Gates discuss events in the Middle East as I glanced at the other cabinet secretaries assembled at the table. Each had ended religious discrimination in their agencies' federal programs, and together they had launched dozens of innovative new partnerships with faith-based and community groups conducting their agencies' business.

When it was my turn to address the cabinet, I charted the progress that they made across federal government agencies to make faith more welcome and human needs more scarce. These accomplishments are detailed in a report called *Quiet Revolution* that is available on Baylor University's Institute for Studies of Religion website.[14] My talented deputy Jedd Medefind served as our office's primary liaison with the agencies and he collaborated with the agency directors to identify the top ten innovations that are enumerated in "Appendix B" and illustrated in the following graphic:

The President's Cabinet and the Compassion Agenda

Cabinet Agency	Human Needs Addressed
United States Agency for International Development	– Social Enterprise in Africa – Combating Malaria – President's Emergency Plan for AIDS Relief (with State Department)
Corporation for National and Community Service	National Service Strategies
Department of Agriculture	– Hunger
Commerce Department	– Inner-city Economic Development – Financial Literacy (with Treasury Department)
Education Department	– School Dropouts – Inner-city Private Schools
Health and Human Services	– Drug Treatment (with Drug Czar) – Mentoring – Healthy Families

---

[14] http://www.baylorisr.org/faithinaction/.

Cabinet Agency	Human Needs Addressed
Homeland Security	– Disaster Preparedness – Immigration Assimilation
Housing and Urban Development	– Homelessness
Justice Department	– Youth Violence – Human Trafficking (co-host with State Department)
Labor Department	– Prisoner Reentry
Small Business Administration	– Nonprofit Capacity Building
Veterans Affairs	– Returning Veterans Care

This progress was not random or voluntary. The president's executive orders established requirements for the agencies' faith-based offices to heighten their outreach to grassroots charities, and Office of Management and Budget (OMB) director Mitch Daniels designed the President's Management Agenda to monitor progress toward these goals.

In a speech given at the site of the 1774 Continental Congress, Bush claimed that government should be citizen-centered, results-oriented, and market-based.[15] Budget director Daniels translated this vision into the PMA's Scorecard to identify key priorities, featuring a red-yellow-green system to register progress on each item. Incorporating the faith-based initiative into the PMA did not attract the same press attention as its legislative strategy to increase tax credits, but it had deep and lasting impact on agency performance. For eight years of the Bush administration, cabinet secretaries were required to report regularly on their progress toward ending discrimination against faith-based groups and adding innovative

---

[15] George W. Bush, "Getting Results from Government" in *Renewing America's Purpose*, June 9, 2000.

programs, such as mentoring children of prisoners and growing public–private partnerships.

The White House's faith-based office operated under the auspices of the Domestic Policy Council, and all policy councils worked under the chief of staff's supervision. Chief of Staff Josh Bolten invited me to brief the president in December 2007 to prepare for the upcoming annual meeting of the nation's governors at the White House. Standard protocol for these briefings features the president in one of the wing chairs in front of the Oval Office fireplace and underneath the George Washington painting. When he attends, the vice president sits in the other wing chair. The briefer sits on the couch nearest the president and opposite the chief of staff, who sits on the couch nearest to the vice president's chair. Other members of the White House staff fill the couches and other chairs brought in near the president's desk.

As I was briefing this day, the decorated Christmas tree behind me, my eyes were locked on the president, who was leaning into my words. However, out of the corner of my eye, I noticed that Vice President Cheney was nodding off. I shot a look to Chief of Staff Bolten, whose wry smile signaled that my content was on course and that I should not be distracted by the dosing veep. I later learned that Cheney suffered from narcolepsy, which lowered my self-consciousness a bit.

Very few people are so relaxed in the Oval Office. I was privileged to host Detroit Tigers ace Justin Verlander for lunch in the West Wing Navy Mess the week following his first major league no-hitter. As former owner of the Texas Rangers, the president loved baseball and invited me to bring Verlander upstairs after lunch. As we stood outside the Oval Office, Verlander looked a little shaky. He told me he was more nervous waiting to enter the Oval Office than he had been in the ninth inning of his no-hitter the previous week. The president regularly observed the same reaction from *Fortune* 500 leaders, so he put his arm around the 6'5" pitcher and warmly welcomed him into the office, where they traded baseball stories for a half hour.

When we welcomed the governors to the White House in early 2008, the president delivered a report depicting the faith-based initiative's footprint in all fifty states. Much like the cabinet meeting, it was deeply rewarding to survey the progress made by these governors in leveling the playing field for faith-based and grassroots charities seeking partnerships with the government, and even more so to see the social innovations taking root in the state and American territories. You can read some of these stories in Chapter 4.

Compassion in Action

Capitalizing on our home field advantage, we hosted Compassion in Action roundtables at the White House each month. This allowed us to demonstrate the fullness of the faith-based initiative's reach. Month after month we tackled such human tragedies as homelessness, youth violence, human trafficking, and the challenges faced by military veterans returning home. Faith-based and community leaders flew in from all around the country each month to help us write a new chapter in the Eisenhower Executive Office Building's (EEOB) history.

This grand building adjacent to the White House was built between 1871 and 1888 to house the war, navy, and state departments. Its flamboyant French Second Empire architecture was patterned after the Louvre's remodeling in 1852, and it stands in stark contrast to the understated monumental buildings across the city. Visitors opening the EEOB's doors grab hold of brass doorknobs carved with the original national security departments formerly housed there. Inside, they roam the halls once walked by Teddy Roosevelt and Franklin Roosevelt as young military aides and Winston Churchill, who charted World War II here.

The strategy we were planning waged battles on a different front. In the president's words, this was a determined attack on need, and the roundtables pursued Compassion in Action's mission by targeting three goals: (1) to declare the most pressing human struggles in America as unacceptable; (2) to highlight the grassroots faith-based and nonprofit innovations solving these problems; and (3) to design better public–private strategies as a result of the conversation.

Mirroring congressional hearings, each of the monthly EEOB events gathered senior government leaders (members of the president's cabinet, Mrs. Bush, and more) alongside scholars, business leaders, and others who offered expert testimony. But the stars of the show were the grassroots innovators themselves who were given the White House stage to tell their stories of helping and healing. Each event featured over 100 leaders specifically recruited for their subject matter expertise. Collectively, we welcomed over 2,000 participants who flew to Washington from across the nation at their own expense.

Full videos of each session and companion materials are available on the Baylor University website referenced earlier. While the Obama administration's faith-based office discontinued the roundtables, they have created a blog to spotlight the federal agency centers' ongoing partnerships with grassroots groups. Since the Bush roundtables covered far more issues than could possibly be discussed in one chapter, the following representative sample highlights three great challenges: natural disasters, drug addiction, and school dropouts.

The First Responders to Disasters

New York's iconic twin towers fell at the hands of terrorists on September 11, 2001. The state of Florida suffered four hurricanes—Charley, Frances, Ivan, and Jeanne—in just six weeks (from August 13, 2004 to September 25, 2004). Hurricane Katrina made landfall in Florida one year later on August 25, 2005, but saved most of its fury for Alabama, Mississippi, and Louisiana. In October 2007, a series of wildfires over a half-billion acres burned from Santa Barbara, California, south to the Mexico border. The subprime mortgage crisis of 2008 has been deemed a "dry flood" by those observing its wreckage on low-income families.

Disasters, whether natural or manmade, visited our shores in epic proportions during the Bush presidency. In our nation's effort to fight back, we transformed the way government—from Washington, D.C., to small-town America—prepares for, responds to, and helps citizens recover from these horrific events. Disaster response was the subject of one of the roundtables I co-hosted with Michael Chertoff, secretary of the Department of Homeland Security (DHS), in 2007.

Secretary Chertoff, who was late arriving to our session because he was held up in an urgent meeting in the White House Situation Room, headed a 200,000-person agency that was formed after 9/11 to create a unified response to disasters and threats. In his remarks to our session, he noted: "Faith-based and community organizations undertake a surprisingly large, varied, and demanding set of initiatives with extraordinary effectiveness, and so we want to do everything we can to harness this energy."[16] He did so formally by

---

[16] Michael Chertoff, keynote remarks from White House Office of Faith-Based and Community Initiatives Compassion in Action Event Series, May 2008.

amending the DHS National Response Framework to integrate the work of faith-based organizations and volunteers.

He also commissioned The Homeland Security Institute to publish an authoritative account of the increased community resiliency resulting from faith-based and community volunteerism efforts. The report found that during "Hurricanes Katrina and Rita, local churches and community organizations—unaffiliated with a national voluntary organization—often served disenfranchised groups that are sometimes missed by more formal response efforts."[17]

All disasters are local, and therefore private voluntary groups are often the first in, last out, and most effective responders. While the United Nations was trying to access Burma during the tragic 2008 cyclone, members of the national Burmese Christian underground church were the true first responders. They received regular airdrops that helped keep the population stable until wider reinforcements arrived. This was the same story that unfolded in 2005 during Katrina, and then was repeated in tornado scenes in Joplin, Missouri, and Moore, Oklahoma. When minutes count, immediate access is a high virtue.

These many small acts of compassion aggregate into an impressive scale. The response to Katrina featured 1 million volunteers who contributed 14 million volunteer hours.[18] The U.S. foundations donated $1 billion to Katrina recovery,[19] which is the most generous corporate response to a domestic natural disaster in history.

Coordinating this citizen-led activity is virtually impossible. By definition, the work of voluntary groups and volun-

---

[17] http://sites.duke.edu/ihss/files/2011/12/Faith-Based_DeskStudyFinalReport_3-16-10.pdf.
[18] Corporation for National and Community Service.
[19] "Giving in the Aftermath of the Gulf Coast Hurricanes," The Foundation Center, 2007.

teers is spontaneous and adaptive to emergent needs. Yet strategic communications is essential for high performance. This reality birthed the Christian Emergency Network (CEN) in 2011, a distribution chain of 300,000 churches, several thousand non-profits, eighty denominations and 250 field reporters. CEN can reach 85 percent of American households within sixty minutes of a major event. During Katrina, the CEN website had 20 million hits per day.[20]

Quick response to disasters is crucial, but the work continues long after the initial hours. Getting individuals back up and running financially after a disaster is an even bigger challenge. This was the message delivered by John Hope Bryant at our Compassion in Action roundtable.[21] Bryant is the founder of Operation Hope, the nation's first nonprofit social investment bank. A social investment bank trades money or in-kind or pro bono professional services for a "hand up" rather than a "handout." Return on investment includes reduced reliance on public subsidies, reduced crime, and increased economic contributions of formerly impoverished citizens.

Post-Katrina, Bryant witnessed the economic disasters that follow natural disasters as he met with families who had car loans but no cars and small business loans but no businesses. In response, FEMA collaborated with Operation Hope to produce Emergency Financial First Aid kits to provide the tools necessary for personal financial recovery post-disaster. These kits offer easy, step-by-step instructions on how to protect personal assets and help users identify and organize key financial records.

---

[20] http://www.christianemergencynetwork.org/about.
[21] Compassion in Action Roundtable, May 19, 2008.

Hal Roark of the Broadmoor Development Corporation in New Orleans also spoke at the roundtable, sharing his organization's creative response post-Katrina. The Broadmoor neighborhood had the unfortunate distinction of being the lowest-lying point in the city. Literally every home in the neighborhood had five feet or more of Katrina's floodwaters filling their first-floor rooms, prompting city planners to propose bulldozing Broadmoor and turn it into a park. Broadmoor's working-class residents, many having evacuated the city, said, "Hands off our homes!" They turned the shock of Katrina into resolve over the injustice of losing their neighborhood for good. They may not be world-class experts in urban planning or disaster relief, but they were experts in their own neighborhood's people and places.

To put that expertise to work, Roark's Broadmoor Development Corporation utilized the Ivy League interns who were flocking to New Orleans for volunteer opportunities. Rather than giving them hammers and paintbrushes, he put them to work at keyboards to modify a software program called Salesforce into a comprehensive registry of the 7,000 residents and 2,400 homes in Broadmoor's neighborhood. With the database operational, volunteers went door-to-door to identify all the community's needs. This enabled donations and volunteer efforts to be targeted like heat-seeking missiles to specific needs. It was more rewarding for donors and volunteers, more beneficial for residents, and more productive for rebuilders. This is the type of bottom-up innovation that is possible among neighborhood entrepreneurs. Roark said that they wanted to be their own cavalry coming over the hill.

The White House released a report, *The Federal Response to Hurricane Katrina: Lessons Learned,* in February 2006. It highlighted the need for government to collaborate more effectively with nonprofits:

> "Even in the best of circumstances, government alone cannot deliver all disaster relief. Often, non-governmental organizations (NGOs) are the quickest means of providing local relief, but perhaps most importantly, they provide a compassionate, human face to relief efforts. We must recognize that NGOs play a fundamental role in response and recovery efforts and will contribute in ways that are, in many cases, more efficient and effective than the Federal government's response. We must plan for their participation and treat them as valued and necessary partners."[22]

The report's wisdom was heeded. Following Katrina, DHS began training faith-based and community groups across the country and educated local officials about their region's nonprofit assets. This effort paid off handsomely during the 2007 California wildfires. The volunteer community provided shelter for nearly 12,000 evacuees and served more than 500,000 meals in shelters and mobile units. This was the first national disaster following the DHS' inclusion of faith-based and volunteerism in the national response framework, and so the director of DHS' faith-based office was embedded in the response-and-recovery nerve center.

Setting the Addicts Free

It is not only natural disasters that bring devastation to families and communities. The scourge of drug addiction also ravages individuals and neighborhoods. According to the *2010 National Survey on*

---

[22] http://georgewbush-whitehouse.archives.gov/reports/katrina-lessons-learned/.

Drug Use and Health by HHS, over six million children live with at least one parent who has a drug addiction. Each year, such addictions cost employers over $122 billion dollars in lost productivity.[23]

Tonja Myles knows a thing or two about addiction and recovery. She was molested at age seven, her mother was an alcoholic, and she went from using drugs in high school to selling them in college. Her life was out of control, and she was contemplating suicide until her grandmother intervened with fervent prayer.

Myles gave her life to Christ and married a pastor named Darren who shared her passion for those suffering in society's shadows. They began their marriage preaching the Good News in the worst drug-infested neighborhoods of Baton Rouge as well as in nursing homes, Salvation Army centers, and any other place they could find others who needed to be set free from their despair. Their inspiration comes from Tonja's life experience and the Bible verse found in John 8:36, "If the Son sets you free, you will be free indeed."

Myles founded the "Set Free Indeed" rehabilitation program at Baton Rouge's Healing Place Church. In 2003, she was among President Bush's special guests at the Capitol to witness the annual State of the Union address live. During the speech, President Bush described the highlights of a new substance abuse treatment program he'd asked the nation's drug czar, John Walters, to design. At the initiative's heart was the aim of closing the gap between those seeking substance abuse treatment and those receiving it. Bush stated:

> "Another cause of hopelessness is addiction to drugs. Addiction crowds out friendship, ambition, moral conviction, and reduces all the richness of life to a single destructive desire.

---

[23] http://www.samhsa.gov/data/NSDUH/2k10NSDUH/2k10Results.htm#1.1.

"As a government, we are fighting illegal drugs by cutting off supplies and reducing demand through anti-drug education programs. Yet for those already addicted, the fight against drugs is a fight for their own lives.

"Too many Americans in search of treatment cannot get it. So tonight I propose a new $600 million program to help an additional 300,000 Americans receive treatment over the next three years.

"Our nation is blessed with recovery programs that do amazing work. One of them is found at the Healing Place Church in Baton Rouge, Louisiana. A man in the program said, 'God does miracles in people's lives, and you never think it could be you.'"

Hearing the president give a "shout out" (her words) to her and Darren's ministry from their couch at home would have been surreal in itself to Myles. But this faithful woman was having a hard time believing that she was actually listening to the address as a guest of the White House, seated next to the First Lady of the United States and gazing at her heroes, Colin Powell and Condoleezza Rice. The whole night was a fairy tale. Yet Myles didn't lose her human touch. As the president entered the House chambers, she noticed Mrs. Bush light up. Later she recounted to the *New York Times* that, even if he's the president, he's "still this nice lady's husband." Myles said she leaned over and said, "I know you're so proud of him," and Mrs. Bush sweetly replied, "I am."

Myles was selected as a White House guest not only for her good work in addiction recovery but also because Set Free Indeed represents the myriad faith-based providers that operate outside of government's view and funding. While the World Health Organization cites spirituality as one of the six domains important to recovery, government was slow to partner with faith-based groups. At the Compassion in Action roundtable, focused on response to addictions, Director Walters explained that the president's program, called Access to Recovery (ATR), sought to cross two divides. In addition to welcoming faith partners for the first time, ATR also bridged treatment and recovery. Drug treatment is offered by clinical professionals and often disconnected from recovery services, yet the two systems of care are essentially dependent on the other.

ATR program director Westley Clark explained at the roundtable that treatment and recovery are irrevocably linked. Whereas the end point of treatment is a disappearance of the clinical disorder, the end point of recovery is holistic health. In other words, when the clinical disorder comes and goes, care is discontinuous. Recovery is a continuous process that works best when interfaced with clinical treatment, if or when necessary.

The value of faith-based programs is their ability to navigate this treatment/recovery divide. The problem for government is that the best faith-based programs do not separate their mission from their message. As detailed in Chapter 6, government can only provide direct funding to faith-based groups that offer their spiritual programs at a different time or place than work being done through taxpayer support. The operative word here is "direct." To protect the religious liberty of those seeking help, government should not impose a faith-based provider through direct funding. But for those individuals who desire to choose a faith-based option, it is constitutional for the government to provide indirect funding though a voucher.

Consequently, Walters and other administration officials designed Access to Recovery as a voucher program to spur a revolution in drug treatment and care. Instead of the government selecting a handful of providers to cover a region, the vouchers enabled dozens or even hundreds of providers to become eligible for participation. This vastly expanded the available pathways to recovery while placing decision-making in the hands of those receiving treatment (a good idea since research shows that positive outcomes increase as individuals are empowered in their recovery). Funding through the ATR was also made more flexible to cover critical supportive components, such as housing aid, that are essential to healing.

By the end of the Bush presidency, ATR had helped some 200,000 individuals in need receive $300 million in rehabilitation and recovery programs offered in dozens of states. We marked this achievement at an ATR Compassion in Action roundtable with remarks from a distinguished-looking gentleman in a dark suit with a master's degree from the University of Michigan. Those qualities made him appear similar to many White House staff members walking the halls of the EEOB, but his other credentials must have lit up Secret Service's computer screens when he passed through the guard station. By the time David Whithers reached age twenty-six, he had been a heroin addict for half his life, and the last time he used drugs he shared a needle with his nephew, who later died from AIDS.

Whithers' faith-based program, Recovery Consultants, targets chronically homeless substance abusers in Atlanta who are 96 percent African American, and 70 percent have had multiple incarcerations. His first office was the hood of a car, where his initial client filled out paperwork after a Narcotics Anonymous meeting. It has grown through a peer-led model and innovations such as Recovery at Work,[24] a social enterprise that employs thirty of his

---

[24] http://www.recoveryatwork.org/ and http://www.recoveryconsultants.org.

clients who otherwise could not find employment because of their prison records.

The ATR voucher program has helped thousands of addicts find the help they need. And in helping them, we are all blessed. As one of the program's federal administrators explained: "Investing in treatment and recovery support not only saves lives, but every dollar invested in treatment and recovery services returns seven dollars in cost savings from social benefits such as recovered health costs, crime, and lost productivity."[25]

Closing the Educational Achievement Gap

Dropping out of high school and participating in gang activity are among the most reliable on-ramps to crime, drug abuse, incarceration, and social exclusion for people like Tonja Myles and David Whithers. Faith-based and community solutions were their remedies, and the Bush White House sought new strategies to prevent these problems from occurring in the first place.

In the spirit of the presidents' citizen-centered legacy described at the start of this chapter, Presidents Clinton, George H.W. Bush, Jimmy Carter, and First Lady Nancy Reagan (representing her husband) joined General Colin Powell in 1997 for a Presidents' Summit for America's Future in Philadelphia. Powell was named chairman of the summit, which also included thirty governors, 100 mayors, and other prominent business leaders. Their combined labor produced five promises that the presidents called upon the nation to fulfill for positive youth development.

General Powell was replaced by his wife Alma as chair of America's Promise due to his service as the nation's first African American secretary of state. Mrs. Powell and America's Promise

---

[25] http://www.samhsa.gov/newsroom/advisories/1010081330.aspx.

CEO Marguerite Kondracke launched the next era with a major initiative aimed at America's dropout crisis. At a White House Compassion in Action roundtable, Powell made her case: The graduation rate in America's fifty largest cities is a paltry 53 percent, meaning that 1.2 million students drop out each year. Research proves that high-school dropouts earn half as much as those who graduate and are twice as likely to live in poverty. Mrs. Powell deemed the crisis a "silent epidemic," and Kondracke announced plans to host similar summits to declare this reality an urgent crisis in all fifty states.

Compounding the dropout crisis is the fact that some of the best urban schools have been closing at alarming rates. Faith-based schools have been a part of the American educational landscape since the Franciscans opened a Catholic school in St. Augustine, Florida, in 1606. The Puritans started schools in the northern colonies soon after, and there were Jewish day schools operating in New York City before the American Revolution. Today, one in six schools grades K–8 in America are faith-based, educating more than 4 million students.

Not only have these schools served many children, they have educated them exceptionally well. Against the backdrop of 47 percent urban school dropouts overall, faith-based schools graduate more than nine in ten of its students. Even though pay is generally lower, teacher quality and commitment is greater, student engagement is higher, and racial harmony is richer.

These results make it especially troubling that thousands of faith-based schools closed their doors since the 1990s. Take Catholic schools, for example. They reached their peak in 1960 at 13,000 schools nationwide, serving more than 5 million kids. Since 1960, more than 5,000 Catholic schools shut down, with some cities being especially hard hit. Detroit and Chicago lost sixty

Catholic schools each from 1998 through 2008 when President Bush convened a national summit to address the crisis.

The event was chaired by Karl Zinsmeister, director of the White House Domestic Policy Council, and organized by White House Fellow Andrew Smarick. They choreographed an impressive roster of scholars and policy experts who provided evidence of the faith factor being present in urban education success rates.[26] This is especially true for minority students, who are 42 percent more likely to complete high school and 250 percent more likely to obtain a college degree if graduating from a Catholic high school rather than a public high school.[27]

Contrary to popular impressions, many of the students in urban Catholic schools are non-Catholic minorities. Over the past several decades, minority enrollment has more than doubled, and non-Catholics have more than tripled. Indeed, it was this emphasis on serving low-income students that contributed to the school closings due to inability to pay and provided much of the rationale for education reformers seeking vouchers or other methods to allow parents to select the best schools for their children, whether public or private.

Former Teach for America vice president Nicole Baker Fulgham found that faith is also a success factor for public school teachers. Fulgham, who joined Mrs. Bush at a White House faith-based conference in New Orleans in May 2008, considers the education gap to be among the leading civil rights challenges of our generation. "A child's zip code shouldn't determine whether he or she is prepared for college," Fulgham argued. "Unfortunately, that disparity is very real; only half of the kids in low-income communities graduate

---

[26] http://georgewbush-whitehouse.archives.gov/infocus/education/whschoolsummit/.
[27] Dale McDonald and Margaret M. Schultz, United States Catholic Elementary and Secondary Schools 2009–2010, National Catholic Educational Association, 2010.

from high school. And those who do graduate are performing, on average, at an eighth-grade level. Kids in wealthier communities are outperforming their counterparts in poorer neighborhoods by three grade levels by the time they reach fourth grade." [28,29]

President Bush, Mrs. Bush, and former education secretary Margaret Spellings have worked together since their days in the Texas governor's office to close this achievement gap. Policy clearly plays an important role to ratchet up instructional quality, hold school leaders accountable for student success, and advance innovation in the classroom. However, they also understand that the work of rescuing dropouts and helping students navigate life's hardships which threaten school success is best done by faith-based and community groups. The Street School Network was one of those groups featured at the presidents' conference. The Network was founded by Tom Tillapaugh in 1984 when he started teaching homeless kids in his home. In his words, he went up to three street kids and said, "Let's go back and have high school." Soon after, he and his wife were housing seven homeless youth, and the city ordered them to shrink it down to two.

Faith-based educational entrepreneurs from around the nation were inspired by Tillapaugh's story and started similar schools themselves. These are schools intentionally kept smaller with teachers that do far more than teach. They have to be *in loco parentis* as well as advocates, dream builders, and mentors. There are dozens of Street Schools in the network, fueled in part by innovative philanthropy such as the Gates Foundation's alternative schools strategy and the Durell Foundation economic literacy model. (The latter is especially powerful since poverty is far more than material.)

[28] White House Conference on Faith Based and Community Initiatives, April 30, 2008.
[29] Nicole Baker Fulgham interview in "Class Action" in *Christianity Today*, July 2010.

The Faith-Based Initiative's Long Tail

The Compassion in Action roundtable events continued month after month, attended by those who were making genuine progress in addressing such diverse needs as the challenges faced by returning military troops, the tragedy of malnourished children worldwide, homelessness in the United States, and gang violence. While we looked at these problems with clear eyes, we did not wring our hands. We celebrated faith-based and other nonprofits that were winning these battles, and we charted new partnerships to expand their reach. We also took this show on the road with dozens of White House national conferences, and we assisted governors with their own state-level events. Collectively, these events trained over 100,000 policymakers and nonprofit leaders across the country. To gauge the range and diversity of our activities, I invite you to look through the lens of my calendar over an eight-week period during the end of 2007 (Appendix C).

President Bush held a two-day national conference in June 2008 attended by 1,500 grassroots nonprofit community leaders. Hundreds more were unable to attend because we couldn't fit them into Washington's largest convention hotel, the Marriott Wardman Park. The faith-based initiative was the subject of then-governor Bush's first major policy speech as a presidential candidate; it was launched via executive order during his first few weeks in office, and it was still being featured in the waning months of his administration.

President Bush's faith-based initiative reshaped government to be more effective in its nonprofit partnerships. It launched dozens of large-scale innovations in the direction of our nation's greatest human needs. Through this initiative, American culture became more welcoming to faith in the public square. My office produced a 105-page report called *Quiet Revolution* that chronicled these accomplishments. We chose the name because the faith-based initiatives' successes existed outside the Washington news cycle. The name was also fitting because America's grassroots innovators do their life-saving work in the obscure corners of society where need resides. They do not seek glory or positive newspaper coverage. Their reward is seeing lives changed and communities restored.

Perhaps we were a little too quiet. Two weeks after our national conference, I received a call from the editor of *USA Today's* editorial page asking if I'd like to write an "Opposing View" to their planned opinion piece in support of presidential candidate Barack Obama's recently announced faith-based initiative. As part of the Obama campaign's self-proclaimed "Values Week," Obama made a brief stop in Zanesville, Ohio, to announce that he would continue the Bush faith-based office.

"Let me get this straight," I replied to the editor. "In a campaign marked by 'Change' as its central theme, Senator Obama just pledged his commitment to sustain the signature domestic policy of the Bush administration, and you want me to write a rebuttal?" Failing to exhibit any sense of the irony, the editor matter-of-factly said, "Yes."

I was pleased the write the piece because it allowed me to acknowledge President Bush's accomplishments. In the 2000 campaign year, the term "faith-based" was first introduced to the national consciousness. Religion was largely associated more with proselytization rather than problem-solving.

Eight years later, "faith-based" had become a ubiquitous term. Today it is used commonly and positively, often in the context of a desired partner in meeting the greatest human needs. This culture change is clearly President Bush's greatest contribution to making America's civic commons more faithful and our society more civil.

In his book, *Giving*, Bill Clinton lauded the Bush faith-based prisoner reentry initiative, Ready4Work, as an important twenty-first-century success story. In his Zanesville speech, Senator Obama cited Ready4Work as the type of innovation his future faith-based office would advance. You can read about this initiative in Chapter 3.

After one term in office, the Obama administration has not only kept its pledge to sustain the Bush faith-based office, they have continued to operate federal agency faith-based centers, including ensuring constitutional protections for faith-based groups. While the Obama faith-based office has not launched the large-scale compassion projects you'll read about in Chapters 3–5, they have continued to emphasize grassroots innovators as the most important part of the government-nonprofit partnership.

> "'Of all the signature initiatives of the Bush era...faith-based initiatives [policy] has managed to survive,' says Lew Daly, a senior fellow at Demos, a New York policy research group. 'That means Bush was onto something about this question of church-state partnerships.'"[30]

From George Washington to Barack Obama, presidents have called on citizens to serve their country by serving their communities. And sometimes those citizens are ex-presidents.

When a tsunami devastated Indonesia in 2004, President Bush recruited his father and former President Clinton to lead the relief effort. And when a hurricane crumbled much of Haiti's capital city of Port-au-Prince in 2010, President Obama enlisted Bill Clinton and George W. Bush to lead the rebuilding effort.

---

[30] http://www.csmonitor.com/USA/Society/2012/0325/A-Bush-era-victory-in-culture-wars-faith-based-initiatives.

Jimmy Carter has reflected that his post-presidency efforts have been more successful than that of his time in office. These days, all former presidents' lives are marked by philanthropy, service, and problem-solving. They form the most exclusive club in the world and have a clubhouse across the street from the White House, furnished with bound volumes of their papers and even a blue rug embroidered with the presidential seal. Plans are underway to transform the former Bush administration's faith-based office into the presidents' new townhouse. This is a fitting gesture memorializing the presidents' call to service and how they continue to live their own lives of giving and serving.

2

THE FAITH FACTOR

As the faith-based initiative was gaining momentum in Washington during the Bush years, many global leaders were still uncertain what to do with it. The fog began to clear when former British prime minister Tony Blair led a panel discussion on "Faith and Modernization" at the World Economic Forum in 2008. The event is better known by the name of its location, Davos, a Swiss village nestled in the Alps. It is regarded as the year's leading fashion show for ideas and celebrity sightings.

Blair is a regular at Davos, but his faith and modernization theme likely struck his peers as an oxymoron since many view religion as a 1950's Eisenhower-era relic rather than an appropriate lens through which to see life in this complex new millennium. Blair however, understands that peace in the Middle East and other human strife remains unsettled when faith questions are not understood and navigated. Toward that end, upon leaving 10 Downing Street he formed the Tony Blair Faith Foundation to promote respect for all the world's religions and to demonstrate the positive effects of faith on the world.

Blair's secret weapon on the panel was a goateed preacher from southern California named Rick Warren. Warren had achieved global renown in his own right thanks to his 22,000-member mega church called Saddleback, which he founded in 1980. Saddleback's growth was fueled in part by its creative worship experience—such as the Easter services held one year at the appropriately named Anaheim Angels stadium. With pop band the Jonas Brothers leading worship, the service drew 45,000 Saddleback friends to hear Warren preach from the pitcher's mound.

Saddleback is about far more than showmanship, though. Each week, approximately 30,000 people (slightly more than attend weekend services) meet for Bible studies and discipleship groups. In 2007, Saddleback took on a goal no other church had ever attempted: they sent 13,000 members to every nation on earth—all 196 countries—to bring health care, literacy programs, orphan care, and the gospel. Additionally, Warren has trained 400,000 pastors worldwide using curriculum based on his bestselling book, *The Purpose Driven Life*, which has sold more than 30 million copies. The book's provocative first sentence, "It's not about you," captures Warren's own outward-focused life and the guiding truth that mobilizes Christians and Warren-followers worldwide to serve others. It's not a perspective one typically finds at the World Economic Forum.

A Faith-Filled Future

At Davos, Warren noted that five-sixths of the world population claims to be religious, or at least spiritual. As such, he argued, leaders cannot address the world's major challenges—pandemic diseases, global poverty, illiteracy, corruption, global warming, and spiritual emptiness—without doing business with the faith factor.

To the skeptical audience, Rick Warren's words were direct and dramatic: "If you're a global business leader, you need to understand that the future is religious pluralism, not secularism. You may not like it, but you have to deal with it. The world is becoming more religious, not less." There are 600 million Buddhists, 800 million Hindus, 1.3 billion Muslims, and 2.3 billion Christians scattered across the globe. The face and shape of religion is not only growing, it's also changing. In China, considered by many to be irreligious, there are more Catholics than in Italy, more Protestants than in England, and more Muslims than in Europe.

Having attended Davos himself in prior years, Warren had heard a lot about public-private partnerships. But these alone seemed like an unstable two-legged stool to him. Though he acknowledged the necessary role of public (government and nonprofit) and private (for-profit) players, Warren noted the equal value faith partners bring in helping solve systemic social problems. "There's no such thing as community development without the church," he told Davos attendees. To make his case, he listed three unique value propositions the church offers:

Universal Distribution—"There are millions of dusty villages scattered across the globe without a business, school, police, or health service, but they have a church," Warren noted. "The church was global 2,000 years before Davos started talking about globalization. And collectively, the church speaks more languages and has 1,000 more people groups than the United Nations."

Largest Pool of Manpower—Hundreds of millions of the faithful serve humanity's needs through their congregations regularly and at no cost. The faith community is the most mobilized and motivated volunteer group on the planet.

Highest Credibility—During the previous year, Warren had completed a 46,000-mile trip in forty-five days, meeting with presidents, prime ministers, and indigenous citizens. He observed that faith leaders held the most credibility at the local level because churches and mosques were there for the long haul. No matter where he traveled, it was the pastor, rabbi, or imam who married, buried, and assisted congregants through life transitions.

Warren loves the church, and he routinely says that his only interest in changing the world is to glorify God. Peace-seekers are motivated to do good for different reasons, he told those assembled at Davos. Some are motivated politically because good deeds promote goodwill; others are motivated by profits because you can do well by doing good; still others are personally motivated because they wish to return the favors they were granted by others. Warren's own reason for doing good? To adhere to his Savior's admonition to love your neighbor as yourself. "Frankly," he said, "I don't care why you do good, as long as you do good."

Before leaving office in 2008, then-president George Bush asked Warren to speak at a global summit on malaria. As Melinda Gates listened to Warren explain the local churches' role in filling the void created by gaps in poor nations' health care systems, she exclaimed: "Now I get it, Rick. Houses of worship can be the distribution center for all that we need to do."[31]

The Role of Faith in Facing Down Global Giants

Melinda Gates' "aha moment" is shared by a wider set of leaders thanks in large part to Warren's tour de force on the world stage. However, it is his church's work in Africa, particularly Rwanda,

---

[31] Rick Warren, quoting Melinda Gates at "Faith and Modernization" session at the Davos World Economic Forum, 2008.

which illuminates the vital and irreplaceable role of faith communities tackling huge international challenges.

Rick Warren does not advocate a private faith or focus his energy on pitting one religion against another. He believes that faith without works is hardly faith at all. His is an active faith that proves its currency by its care and compassion. Jesus told his disciples that the world will know they were his followers by the love they show for one another.

In 2002, it was Rick Warren's wife, Kay, who taught him many of these lessons. During her courageous recovery from cancer, she stumbled onto a magazine article about the 12 million children orphaned in Africa because of AIDS. The article haunted her, so much so that she described herself as "a seriously disturbed woman." Unable to erase the images of horrific suffering from her mind, she traveled to Africa to see the problem firsthand and figure out what she could do to help. Rick went along to support his wife. Little did he know he was about to discover his own life's next big assignment there.

In South Africa, Warren met a rural pastor whose church met under a tree. As he approached the pastor, the man excitedly greeted him. "I know who you are! You're Pastor Rick." He then explained how he walked three hours each week to download Warren's sermons at the nearest post office.

In tearful response, Warren committed to using his leadership gifts to equip bush pastors like the man before him. Inspired by this exchange, Warren asked God what other problems he wanted him to tackle next.

After returning from his first trip to Africa, Warren pored over eighteen pages of notes which revealed the five global problems that were chiefly responsible for trapping the bottom billion worldwide in extreme poverty. What emerged was an acrostic—the PEACE

Plan, an audacious vision that paired the world's greatest challenges with solutions the church is uniquely positioned to solve.

Problem	Solution
Spiritual emptiness: "People don't know God made them for a purpose."	**P. Plant** new churches or partner with existing ones
Egocentric leadership: "The goal of leadership is not how many people serve you, but how many people you help."	**E. Equip leaders**
Poverty: "Half the world lives on less than $2 per day."	**A. Assist the poor**
Disease: "Billions of people suffer from preventable diseases."	**C. Care for the sick**
Illiteracy: "Half the world is functionally illiterate."	**E. Educate the next generation**

The PEACE Plan would not be a top-down, experts-driven strategy. Instead, it would be a model like the one described in Luke 10, centered on sending ordinary (emphasis on *ordinary*) people out in teams in search of people of peace to join them in their work. Warren knew there weren't enough doctors, teachers, and other professionals to combat his global giants. But he also knew that there were millions of volunteers—an army of believers—stationed in millions of churches worldwide with the technology to connect electronically. They simply lacked the vision and capacity to mobilize.

By calling all of God's people to make a difference wherever they were, Warren addressed two problems at the same time: bringing help to the needy and releasing the latent energy of a church that had been sitting idle for too long. In other words, both global poverty and apathy can be defeated when effective partnerships fuse the world's biggest needs with the church's leading strengths. Billy Graham has called Warren's PEACE Plan "the greatest, most comprehensive, and most biblical vision for world missions I have ever heard or read about."[32]

PEACE in Rwanda

Saddleback launched the PEACE Plan in phases, much like NASA approached its mission to put a man on the moon. The goal of Mercury, the first rocket sent into space, was to successfully leave the earth's atmosphere. Gemini sought to orbit the globe. Apollo's mission was to make it to the moon and back again.

Similarly, Saddleback tackled its mission to reach every nation with the PEACE Plan by first sending people from the church to every country on the planet. For most of these suburban American missionaries, traveling to foreign lands and experiencing different cultures was like Mercury's leaving the earth's atmosphere. As his California congregation focused on getting to know people in all corners of the world, Warren continued to look for ways to mobilize the church worldwide to best utilize its ubiquitous locations, outsized pool of manpower, and paramount credibility of its leaders.

Then came an invitation from Paul Kagame, president of Rwanda. He wanted Warren to teach the pastors in his country how to lead with purpose. Kagame had been personally transformed by Warren's *Purpose Driven Life,* and he believed the book's principles, if followed, would be Rwanda's best chance to lift itself out of

---

[32] David Van Biema, "Rick Warren Goes Global," *Time,* May 27, 2008.

poverty and eliminate the diseases that threatened its survival. This was Warren's chance to test-drive his PEACE Plan.

Two months after his appearance at Davos with Tony Blair, Warren addressed a White House faith-based conference that I co-hosted in Rwanda with President Kagame to promote public-private partnerships. Warren spoke of Saddleback's community health project in the Western Province. This region is home to 70,000 people, but there are only three hospitals and eighteen clinics in locations requiring a one- or two-day walk for most people. In contrast to this sparse smattering of medical facilities, the Western Province is home to 869 churches—each one within a five-minute walk of another.

With an eye toward leveraging the close proximity of each church to the communities that lacked access to health care, Warren traveled to Rwanda with a group of volunteers from Saddleback. They met with local pastors and asked each one if they wanted to select two members from their church to be trained in administering basic medical treatment to the people in their community. Eight pastors said yes. The first sixteen volunteers learned how to wash hands, boil water, dry sheets in the sun, dress and stitch a wound, and administer antiretroviral drugs (ARV) to HIV/AIDS patients. These sixteen volunteers soon grew to eighty, then 360, and so on. After only twenty-four months, more than 3,000 church volunteers in Rwanda had been trained as health care providers, which included home visits each day to the seven families assigned to each of them.

From one of the world's most under-resourced nations medically to a country that now features a church-based health care center within a five-minute radius from any location, Warren's experiment in Rwanda highlights the power of the church to create an effective distribution method to care for the sick.

Warren's speeches and strategies have inspired experts like Boston College sociologist Alan Wolfe to credit him with changing the church's brand. In a *Wall Street Journal* article, Wolfe noted: "Historians are likely to pinpoint Mr. Warren's trip to Rwanda as the moment conservative evangelical Protestantism made questions of social justice central to its concerns."[33]

Warren himself, however, would point out that compassion has been a part of the Christian church's character since its founding. And that matters, for at least two reasons.

One is that cynics—who have to admit to seeing some progress among U.S. congregations towards a greater external focus—might wish to argue that a social justice consciousness is merely a passing fad. The other is that some religious leaders are reluctant to fully commit themselves to the compassion mandate, and they desperately need to recover and remember their tradition's own long and beautiful history.

The story of faith-filled compassion has ancient roots. Judaism, Islam, and Christianity all exhort adherents to generosity and service. The Christian tradition finds its most inspiring model in the life of Jesus Christ himself.

The Church Invents Compassion

Compassion was central to Jesus' ministry, and the Scriptures reveal that his mercy toward the sick, hungry, and hurting people he encountered was always followed by an action verb. Consider these three verses from the New Testament:

Matthew 14:14—Jesus *had compassion on them and healed their sick* ...

[33] Alan Wolfe, "A Purpose-Driven Nation? Rick Warren Goes to Rwanda," *The Wall Street Journal*, August 26, 2005.

Matthew 20:34—Jesus *had compassion on them and touched their eyes....*

Mark 8:2—Jesus *has compassion on the crowd and fed* 4,000 (paraphrase) ...

In his landmark book, *The Triumph of Christianity*, historian Rodney Stark writes that Rome was subjected to a deadly plague in the middle of the third century. The toll was horrific—5,000 people died every day in Rome alone, their bodies heaped up in piles. Family members fled to protect their lives, but the Christians stayed to care for the dying members of the pagans' families and acted as custodians for the dead.

Bishop Dionysius of Alexandria reported, "Heedless of danger, [the Christians in Rome] took charge of the sick, attending to their every need, and ministering to them in Christ. And with them departed this life serenely happy, for they were infected by others with the disease, drawing on themselves the sickness of their neighbors, and cheerfully accepting their pains."[34] Stark quotes the historian Paul Johnson who said, "The Christians ... ran a miniature welfare state in an empire which for the most part lacked social services."[35]

Stark comments that this upside-down behavior frustrated the plans of the Emperor Julian, who sought to displace the growing Christian church with Neoplatonic paganism in the fourth century. In reaction to the favor granted these charitable Christ-followers, Julian commanded pagan priests to distribute wine and grain to the poor. However, his plans proved futile when the Christians provided support to the pagans as well; this

---

[34] Rodney Stark, *The Rise of Christianity* (San Francisco: Harper Collins, 1997), 83.
[35] Ibid., 113.

left the pagan priests without any tradition to associate with such others-centeredness.

Soon after Julian's death in 363 AD, St. Gregory of Nyssa and his brother Basil had an idea. Instead of shunning the leper community, they would care for them at no charge. The First Council of Nicaea (best known for its Nicene Creed) convened in 325 AD and ordered the construction of a hospital in every cathedral town to care for the sick, widows, and strangers. Basil, who served as bishop of Caesarea, complied with this charge by building a massive structure that included housing for medical staff and a separate section for lepers. This type of facility became known as a *basilica*.

The early church went beyond simply meeting material needs. Following Jesus' commandment to love one's neighbor as oneself, the church fathers instructed their followers not to stigmatize the poor or the sick. Not only did a leper suffer the severe pain of his ailment, he suffered still more when people couldn't bear to even look upon him or be near him. The latter is a heavier burden to bear.

St. Gregory, who helped to raise money for his brother's project, addressed the human toil in what is considered one of the finest homilies of his era:

> "Lepers have been made in the image of God.... In the same way you and I have, and perhaps preserve that image better than we, let us take care of Christ while there is still time. Let us minister to Christ's needs. Let us give Christ nourishment. Let us clothe Christ. Let us gather Christ in. Let us show Christ honor."[36]

---

[36] St. Gregory of Nyssa, "On the Love of the Poor," sermon.

Fast-forward 1,400 years to eighteenth-century England. John Wesley wrote the last letter of his life to William Wilberforce, exhorting the evangelical Christian and member of Parliament to sustain his campaign to end slavery across the British Empire. Wesley himself took on the cause of prison reform. Prisons in that time were dark, dirty, and overcrowded. Dangerous criminals and debtors were housed with men, women, and children kept in chains. There was no care for the sick. When Wesley visited his first prison in 1730 with his brother Charles, he said, "What a scene appears as soon as you enter! The very place strikes horror into your soul. How dark and dreary! How unhealthy and unclean! How void of all that might minister comfort!"[37]

He returned each week to Newgate Prison in London to bring such comfort by educating and ministering to the inmates. Scripture's command to love God with all your heart, mind, and soul, and to love your neighbor as yourself inspired Wesley to make prison visitation a hallmark of the church and the movement he led. "By doing good ... by giving food to the hungry, by clothing the naked, by visiting or helping them that are sick or in prison"—this was a rule from the General Rules of the United Societies of 1743 that Wesley lived out. He understood that compassion ministry was essential to growing as a disciple of Christ.

Similar faith-filled missions led to the establishment of some of the world's greatest charities in the nineteenth and twentieth centuries, such as the Red Cross, YMCA, Salvation Army, United Way, and Goodwill Industries. Of the $300 billion donated to charity in America each year in the modern era, 32 percent is directed

---

[37] John Wesley, *The Works of the Reverend John Wesley, A.M.* (New York: B. Waugh and T. Mason, 1835) p.122.

to religious causes. The second ranking recipient is educational institutions at a distant 14 percent.[38]

Faith as Foreign Policy

The faith community is not merely a distributor of social goods, as important as its contributions to community and individual well-being are. Religious institutions and commitments have huge cultural and political implications. Part of any "faith-based initiative" is attentiveness to the public significance of faith—whether that means an appreciation of its social benefits or its role in shaping people's attitudes on a wide range of social and political issues. In other words, taking faith seriously is part of the faith-based initiative. But, as Warren noted in his talk at Davos, many political leaders ignore faith. This is to their peril.

As mentioned at the beginning of this chapter, one international statesman who has not made that mistake is former British prime minister Tony Blair. However, he discovered within his own administration that such religious literacy and appreciation were easily dismissed. Blair once told his speechwriters that he wanted to end one of his addresses to the nation with "God bless Britain," much like all US presidents end with "God bless America." His top political aide, Alistair Campbell, bluntly shot down the idea, reminding him that Britain was not America. "We don't do God," Campbell sniffed.[39]

Missing the irony that England has a state-sponsored church, Blair followed Campbell's advice and cloaked his faith during his time in office out of fear that Britons would consider him a "nutter" if he sounded religious. Upon leaving office, Blair converted to

[38] *Giving USA 2012: The Annual Report on Philanthropy for the Year 2011.*
[39] http://www.telegraph.co.uk/news/uknews/1429109/Campbell-interrupted-Blair-as-he-spoke-of-his-faith-We-dont-do-God.html.

Catholicism (his wife Cherie's faith tradition) and set up the Tony Blair Faith Foundation[40] in tandem with his role as Envoy to the Quartet on the Middle East. The Quartet includes leaders from the United Nations, the European Union, the United States, and Russia. Together this coalition addresses the escalating conflict in the Middle East. As special envoy, Blair is acutely aware how much the region does indeed "do God."

The Blair Faith Foundation's overarching objective is to deepen understanding of the world's religions and demonstrate how faith can be a powerful force for good in the modern world. The foundation deals with the reality that religious faith is vitally important to billions of people worldwide, and its overriding manifestation is compassion and justice.

To illustrate, Blair likes to tell the story of the great Jewish sage, Rabbi Hillel, who lived in Israel during the first century BC. A prospective convert to Judaism once challenged Hillel to teach him the entire Torah while standing on one leg. Hillel passed the test with his pithy retort, "That which is hateful unto you do not do to your neighbor. This is the whole of the Torah; the rest is commentary. Go forth and study."[41]

For Blair, the story succinctly shows how all major faith traditions feature a central tenet to love neighbors as self. His foundation seeks to inform leaders and global citizens through its Faith and Globalization Initiative, which he highlighted at the Davos conference during his joint appearance with Rick Warren. He is also educating the next generation through a course at Yale University, as well as an innovative "Face to Faith" program in

---

[40] http://www.tonyblairfaithfoundationus.org.
[41] http://www.myjewishlearning.com/texts/Rabbinics/Talmud/Mishnah/Mishnah_and_its_Times/Hillel.shtml; Shabbat 31a, *Talmud.*

schools from nineteen countries that links fourteen-year-olds of different faiths via video technology.

Yet illiteracy of religion is not the only problem. There are some who do harm in the name of religion, as depicted in Samuel Huntington's 1993 *Foreign Affairs* essay, "The Clash of Civilizations." Huntington's theory is that cultural and political allegiances will drive the major sources of conflict in the post–Cold War era. Traditional frameworks of politics and economics will no longer be reliable in understanding or managing the type of sectarian conflicts witnessed in places like Bosnia and Iraq. Cultural and political acumen is required for navigating this complex civil, religious, and tribal terrain.

A late convert to this thinking is former U.S. secretary of state Madeline Albright who had only heard God in respect (i.e., "godless communists") during most of her academic and diplomatic life. Now, however, she is often quoted as saying such things as, "If you think Jerusalem is just a piece of real estate, you're never going to get it right."[42]

Albright translated this sentiment into remarks to the Yale Divinity School in 2004[43] where she quoted from then vice president Dick Cheney's Christmas card bearing inscription, "If a sparrow cannot fall to the ground without His notice, is it probable that an empire can rise without His aid?" The speech's popularity inspired her to build out these themes further in a book called *The Mighty and Almighty: Reflections on America, God and World Affairs.*[44]

---

[42] "Albright: Ignore religion 'at our own peril'" on CNN.com, August 21, 2007.

[43] http://yaledailynews.com/blog/2004/03/31/former-secretary-of-state-rejects-view-of-god-as-teammate-in-war.

[44] Madeline Albright, *The Mighty and Almighty: Reflections on America, God and World Affairs* (New York: Harper, 2006).

Among her insightful observations is the "borderless nature of religious faith often makes it easier for leaders to talk to one another, easier for nations to agree on common values."[45] In the post-9/11 world, religion can no longer be separated from international relations and diplomacy must be shaped by morality.

> "The borderless nature of religious faith often makes it easier for leaders to talk to one another; easier for nations to agree on common values; and easier for people from vastly different backgrounds to reach a consensus about moral standards."
> —Madeleine K. Albright, *The Mighty and the Almighty: Foreign Policy and God*

Douglas Johnston is the originator of what has become known as the faith-based diplomacy movement. To understand the likes of Osama bin Laden and Slobodan Milošević, both of whom were religious demagogues who turned misshapen theology into mass terror, one must understand the ideas behind their guns. However, Johnson explains two reasons why American policy-makers are not up to the task. First, the foreign policy apparatus in Washington has seen the separation of church and state as an excuse not to understand those who do not separate the two. And second, the same decision-makers have for too long relied on the rational actor theory of international relations, which has no place for religion.

General Anthony Zinni agrees with Johnson that religious literacy is among the most sophisticated tools in the diplomat's toolkit. Simply put, religion must be part of the solution when it is part of the problem. In the foreword to Johnston's latest book,

---

[45] "Albright: Ignore religion 'at our own peril'" on CNN.com, August 21, 2007.

Religion, Terror, and Error: US Foreign Policy and the Challenge of Spiritual Engagement, Marine Corps General, Commander-in-Chief of the U.S. Central Command, and U.S. Special Envoy to the Middle East Zinni wrote this about faith-based diplomacy:

> "This is a visionary approach that goes beyond the whole of government effort and which expands the current definition of smart power. From my two decades of experience in the Islamic world, I am convinced the vast majority of Muslims would embrace this approach as a means to clearly express their beliefs and enabling them to understand ours."[46]

South Africa following apartheid offers a glimpse into a grassroots version of type of faith-based diplomacy; in this case, a bottom-up case of Pentecostal churches fashioning democratic participation from the formerly marginalized black population. Prior to arriving at the White House, I joined Boston University sociologist Peter Berger in studying the role of Pentecostal churches in rural areas outside of Johannesburg in building social capital.

Our report found that the rural South African Pentecostal churches expanded the role of women in society and promoted entrepreneurship, a strong work ethic, and the education of all children. As little platoons of democracy, they also were places where the poor learned how to function in a democracy by participating in church meetings, budget planning, and setting priorities. This enabled not only the formerly marginalized groups to be included in society, but the churches' teaching on delayed gratification, savings, and strong families empowered them to be self-sufficient and

---

[46] Douglas Johnston, *Religion, Terror, and Error: U.S. Foreign Policy and the Challenge of Spiritual Engagement* (Santa Barbara, Calif.: Praeger, 2011).

even prosperous. This offers hope that the true African Renaissance would emerge from civil society rather than the politicians.

The Evidence of a Faith Factor

So, the previous two sections made the case that taking faith seriously means recognizing the faith community's contributions to the common good and the importance of understanding the impact of faith in global affairs. Now we'll turn our attention to the inherent power of faith to catalyze personal transformation. Public sector partnerships to solve community problems include faith institutions, but their inclusion shouldn't be merely because churches are located in the right places (convenient to the need), trusted by neighbors, or able to mobilize large numbers of people and big amounts of resources. We need to include faith-based groups because their faith-based approach to individual change is effective.

The First Lady doesn't typically join her husband in West Wing meetings, but George and Laura Bush sat in front of the five military flags prominent in the Roosevelt Room to hear scholars Robert Putnam and Arthur Brooks talk about the effect religion has on our society.

Putnam, a Harvard sociologist and author of the landmark book, *Bowling Alone*,[47] asserted that America's religious landscape has deeply enriched our social capital. In contrast to the waning civic participation he found among Americans in his earlier research, he studied places like Saddleback Church's small group ministry to determine if religious life positively impacts public life. This empirical research was later published in a book he co-authored

---

[47] Robert Putnam, *Bowling Alone: The Collapse and Revival of American Community* (New York: Touchstone Books, 2001).

with David Campbell called *American Grace*.[48] Putnam's conclusion: Religion is the number one predictor of giving and serving in America.

Syracuse economist Arthur Brooks expanded on the theme of religion and its effect on giving and serving; his research found that 91 percent of the faithful are charitable givers compared to 66 percent of givers who do not claim a religious affiliation.[49] Brooks' message is clear: Giving is healthy; it promotes character formation, and is therefore pro-social.

Science indicates that giving is also part of creation. Much has been made about the "helper's high"—pleasure-producing opioids are released when we give or serve. Such rewards from the brain motivate repeated behavior, causing a virtuous cycle to generate. By contrast, Brooks jokes, this kind of endorphin rush rarely occurs when paying one's tax bill.

Putnam and Brooks' observations are echoed by other contemporary researchers, such as Rodney Stark, whose book, *America's Blessings*, attributes a $2.6 trillion annual net benefit to society from religious behavior.[50] Also, the University of Pennsylvania's Ram Cnaan found that a sample of 2,000 congregations in Philadelphia produced $250 million value to the community annually.[51] He refers to this benevolence as the invisible caring hand. Like the Christmas classic *It's a Wonderful Life*, we wouldn't want to see the state of our cities without its benefits.

[48] Robert Putnam and David Campbell, *American Grace: How Religion Divides and Unites Us* (New York: Simon & Schuster, 2012).

[49] Arthur C. Brooks, "Religious Faith and Charitable Giving" *Policy Review*, October 1, 2003.

[50] Rodney Stark, *America's Blessings: How Religion Benefits Everyone, including Atheists* (West Conshohocken, PA: Templeton Press, 2012).

[51] Ram Cnaan, *The Other Philadelphia Story: How Local Congregations Support Quality of Life in Urban America* (Philadelphia: University of Pennsylvania Press, 2006).

David Larson is considered by many to be the pioneer of "faith factor" research. A psychiatrist and epidemiologist with the National Institutes of Health for much of his career, Larson established the National Institute for Healthcare Research (NIHR) to analyze the intersection of spirituality and religion in health outcomes. Previous to Larson's research, faith was viewed as mere sentiment or superstition by the scientific community. Indeed, the term "mind–body" was never even used when Larson was a medical student.

Then came the avalanche of studies through NIHR that drew positive correlations between religious worship and a reduction in stress, addictive behavior, high blood pressure, and psychiatric symptoms for those suffering from mental health disorders. His findings also revealed a correlation between habitual prayer and religious commitment and improved recovery rates and shortened hospital stays. As a result of Larson's work, more than half of the medical schools in America now offer courses on religion and health outcomes, and a Duke University lecture series was established in his honor. Jeff Levin was selected to deliver the inaugural David B. Larson Memorial Lecture, and he continues to lead the health and faith research field at Baylor.

Beyond health care, Larson expanded his faith factor research by joining then–Vanderbilt University criminologist Byron Johnson in original research and a review of the academic literature on reducing crime among youth. They concluded what many grandmothers have known for a long time: Religion keeps kids out of trouble.

One of Johnson and Larson's studies in the mid-1990s found that participation in religious services significantly lowered the likelihood that young black males would use or sell drugs. This brings to mind the allegory of someone being confronted by a gaggle of nineteen-year-old men who suddenly appeared from an alley at 10:00 p.m. on a lonely New York City street. Would that person be comforted to know that the young men had just left a Bible study?

Johnson, now as director of the Institute for Studies of Religion at Baylor University where I am affiliated, has continued to research the faith factor in criminal justice. In his recent book called *More God, Less Crime*,[52] he explains that churches that offer mentoring relationships to protect against external pressures and incorporate faith precepts help youth to become more resilient.

During President Bush's first term, it was Johnson who briefed the president in the Roosevelt Room. The subject was his recently completed evaluation of Chuck Colson's faith-based prisoner rehabilitation program, Innerchange. Its success motivated the president to announce a Prisoner Reentry Initiative in his 2004 State of the Union address. That story is told in the next chapter.

---

[52] Byron Johnson, *More God, Less Crime: Why Faith Matters and How It Could Matter More* (West Conshohocken, PA: Templeton Press, 2011).

3

TO RESCUE AND RESTORE

Those who live in the shadows of society—the prisoner paying his debt to society, the teenager forced into a gang or stolen from parents to work in a third-world brothel, or the woman abused by a husband who promised to love her—suffer not only pain but hopelessness. It seems that the world has either forgotten them, or worse, deemed them unfit for rescue or restoration.

Into this void step courageous volunteers, charities, and caring neighbors who shine their light in some very dark places. It was exactly this type of healers who President Bush designed the faith-based initiative to support. This chapter presents a justice cluster of sorts, providing a snapshot of the faith- and community-based partners that serve prisoners, troubled teens, and abused women.

It was a paradox for the president's motorcade to arrive at a prisoner reentry facility located along the same Baltimore streets used to film the HBO gang-and-drugs series called *The Wire*. On the day following President Bush's last State of the Union address in January 2008, spending a full day at a hardscrabble inner-city neighborhood in the company of two dozen men whom society would prefer to forget was not in the White House communications team's script. But it was in the president's heart.

"Fellas, I'm here to tell you that America is a land of second chances," said President Bush to the men of the Jericho re-entry project. Those assembled were understandably reticent to speak in the president's company, so he broke the ice by saying, "You know, the Book I read says the first will be last and the last will be first." Then he told them that they shared some common struggles. "You've heard of the twelve-step program, haven't you?" inquired the President. They nodded. "Well, I had a two-step program. I found Jesus, and I quit drinking."

One man among the group listening to this new rendition of the Texas two-step was Julius.[53] He sheepishly remarked that meeting a president was the most exciting moment in his life but that the experience was marred because he had to spend the time talking about his biggest failures. He went on to explain how he was starting over and how he desperately wanted his daughter to know the new version of himself.

When facing the national press an hour later, the president was prepared to give a summary of his prisoner reentry initiative and the good work being done at Jericho. White House speechwriters had included Julius' story in the prepared remarks, and of course it would be necessary to spell out his failures in order for the press to appreciate how far he'd come. As the president turned to the talking points about Julius' journey from drug dealer to re-engaged dad, I could sense his mind flashing back to the intimate exchange just moments earlier. And as Bush was himself the father of daughters, I had observed in earlier instances how tender he became when promoting the virtues of fatherhood and healthy families. Now, before the assembled press, I could tell he was envisioning Julius' daughter watching the speech, and he didn't want to rehearse Julius'

---

[53] Name changed to protect identity.

crimes. Like a quarterback calling an audible, the president lowered his cards and went off script.

With Julius standing at his side, Bush skipped over the prepared text and shared instead how he was a lot like the men at this facility. Then he repeated his earlier exchange with them about his own life struggles, this time before the cameras. I immediately surveyed the press pool and noticed that they had found their news hook; headlines in papers coast-to-coast the following day reported on his visit with this headline: "At Faith-Based Event, Bush Recalls Drinking Problem."[54]

To the press, Julius' story was predictable, and the good work being done at this facility was impressive but not newsworthy. But a president of the United States reflecting on his own battles sold newspapers. So on the day following his last State of the Union address, the president traded a day's worth of good news for some bad articles. What did he get in exchange? A family blessed by another step in the father's recovery.

We were not there to win political points in the afterglow of the previous night's State of the Union address. We were meeting with men who lost their voting rights and were hidden—if not despised—by society. We were not there to highlight our success but rather these men's significance. President Bush's kindness to Julius and his willingness to forfeit his media message for human dignity is among the many untold stories of his presidency.

It was also an unlikely story given that he was the leader of a political party known more for "lock 'em up" than help them out. Successful politicians in the 1970s through the 1990s often campaigned on a "get tough on crime" message. Republicans

---

[54] "At faith-based event, Bush recalls drinking problem," http://www.reuters.com/article/2008/01/29/us-bush-faith-idUSN2962792620080129.

Richard Nixon, Ronald Reagan, and George H.W. Bush, as well as Democrat Bill Clinton, each made the issue a key plank in their road to the White House. Violent crime had become a menacing problem over the past several decades, prompting judges and lawmakers to fill the jails with new laws like "three strikes" (imposing sentences of twenty-five years to life for persons convicted of three or more serious crimes) and a war on drugs.

The result was double to triple increases in jail and prison populations during the Nixon to Clinton administrations. From 1974 to 2001, the United States saw a 1.1 million increase in the number of adults in prison; up from 216,000—a five-fold increase! By the new millennium, America had 5 percent of the world's population, but it was holding 25 percent of the world's prisoners. There are approximately 1.5 million criminals behind bars at any given time, and roughly 650,000 are released each year. The cost associated with our prison system is staggering. Annual prison costs are approximately $60 billion. Conservatively, the cost of housing a prisoner each year is $25,000.[55,56,57,58]

A Heart for Restorative Justice

Due to policies aimed primarily at maintaining order in the facilities, there has been more attention focused on restraint than rehabilitation. For example, contact with the outside world is significantly restricted for inmates to protect against contraband being smuggled in. The unintended consequences of this policy is that

[55] Thomas P. Bonczar, "Prevalence of Imprisonment in the U.S. Population, 1974–2001" Bureau of Justice Statistics Special Report, 2003.

[56] Adam Liptak, "Inmate Count in U.S. Dwarfs Other Nations'" *The New York Times*, April 23, 2008.

[57] E. Ann Carson and Daniela Golinelli, "Prisoners in 2012—Advance Counts" Bureau of Justice Statistics, July 25, 2013.

[58] United States Department of Justice.

prisoners become increasing isolated from healthy outside influences and more acclimated to the values and behavior of fellow inmates.

The current system also falls short when it comes to prisoner reentry. The typical prison reentry program gives ex-convicts $100 upon release and a one-way bus ticket back to the same social network that helped them get in trouble the first time. They are also met with unemployment and housing discrimination, compounded by their often-limited job skills and frequently their substance abuse or mental health problems. It's not surprising, therefore, that two-thirds of these former inmates are arrested for new crimes within three years of their release from prison. The wasted lives are tragic, and this formula makes for unstable communities when they're out and continued swelling prison populations when they're in.

George W. Bush acquired a passion for restorative justice during his days in Texas as a young aviator for the Texas Air National Guard in Houston, where he flew Convair F-102s with the 147th Reconnaissance Wing. Bush was recruited by former Houston Oiler tight end John White to be a mentor at an inner-city nonprofit called Project PULL (Professional United Leadership League). "It was tragic, heartbreaking, and uplifting, all at the same time," said Bush. "I saw a lot of poverty. I also saw bad choices: drugs, alcohol abuse, men who fathered children and walked away leaving single mothers struggling to raise children on their own." Then he found out that a young boy from PULL named Jimmy was killed in a gang shooting. Bush said this boy had been "like a little brother." His heartbreak was profound.[59]

When he became the governor of Texas twenty years later, Bush made juvenile justice reform one of his top four priorities. He returned to Houston as governor to tour a Prison Fellowship

---

[59] George W. Bush, *A Charge to Keep: My Journey to the White House* (New York: HarperCollins Publishers, 1999), 58.

program, the InnerChange Freedom Initiative, during its first year of operation. The prisoner reentry program offered Bible study, job training, and mentoring as a pathway to preparing for life outside the prison walls. Swept up in the moment, Governor Bush joined a group of fifty-five prison inmates in a rousing chorus of "Amazing Grace."[60] He joined arms with a forty-six-year-old inmate named George Mason, a convicted murderer. It was not the only time the two would meet. As president, Bush was able to give Mason a hug when Mason visited the White House to participate in a briefing on the InnerChange program's success in restoring ex-offender's lives.

The InnerChange Freedom Initiative was tested in the Jester II Unit (nicknamed "God Pod"), and it became the signature effort by Prison Fellowship's founder Chuck Colson, who observed a similar model achieving remarkable results in Brazil. Colson himself knew about second chances. A presidential aide in Nixon's law-and-order White House, armed with service in the Marines, an Ivy League education, and a law degree, Colson thought his only flaw was pride. That changed on July 9, 1974, when he spent his first night in prison for his role in attempting to cover up the Watergate burglary. Prior to incarceration, his friend from politics, Raytheon chairman Tom Phillips, gave Colson a copy of C.S. Lewis' *Mere Christianity*. This book was instrumental in leading Colson to become a practicing Christian while in prison.[61]

Colson's religious conversion was greeted with widespread skepticism at first, but he lived a post-prison life marked by authentic witness, integrity between his beliefs and action, and a relentless love for the downtrodden, especially the prisoners who, like him, would be marked by their prison number for the rest of their lives.

[60] Ibid., 215.

[61] Charles W. Colson, *Born Again* (Grand Rapids: Baker Publishing Group, 2008).

His desire to give other prisoners the inner joy and transformation he experienced, even while being "on the inside" behind bars, gave InnerChange its name and mission.

Colson went on to become a successful author and renowned Christian leader. He went far beyond public redemption to win the $1 million Templeton Prize for religion. He donated the money to his ministry, Prison Fellowship, and raised many millions more over a quarter century following its founding. He recruited tens of thousands to work in more than two-thirds of America's prisons, and he used his conservative credentials and political savvy to change "lock 'em up" policies to a restorative justice approach that prevented crime and redeemed prisoners' lives so that they could make a healthy return to society.[62]

More God, Less Crime

Dr. Byron Johnson, whose Baylor University research team I joined after leaving Washington, D.C., was invited to the White House in June 2003 along with Prison Fellowship founder Chuck Colson to present an evaluation of the InnerChange program Bush had visited five years earlier. Johnson's research revealed that InnerChange program graduates were rearrested at an 8 percent rate, far lower than the 20 percent recidivism rate of the inmate control group.[63]

President Bush liked what he saw of InnerChange when visiting the new program as Texas governor. Now, as president, he wanted to extend its benefits to prisoners across the country. On

---

[62] Tim Weiner, "Charles W. Colson, Watergate Felon Who Became Evangelical Leader, Dies at 80," *New York Times* (April 21, 2012).

[63] Since the 2003 release of Johnson's research on InnerChange, Grant Duwe and Byron Johnson conducted a cost-benefit analysis of the InnerChange program in a Minnesota prison. This 2013 study not only found the InnerChange program effective in reducing recidivism, but also found that it saved Minnesota taxpayers more than $8,300 per participant (http://www.lifescienceglobal.com/home/cart?view=product&id=642).

January 20, 2004, Bush delivered his State of the Union address, which included these words: "America is the land of the second chance, and when the gates of prison open, the path ahead should lead to a better life."[64] He then proposed a four-year, $300 million Prisoner Reentry Initiative to help ex-convicts get help with jobs, housing, and life skills. This would become one of many "second chance" government-funded start-ups whose roots grew out of President Bush's own faith.

Prisoner reentry affects all Americans. Its success or failure has implications for public safety, the welfare of children, family unification, and community health, and its challenges are significant. Employers typically view ex-offenders as a severe liability. If they were to commit a crime on the job, business owners could face a lawsuit that would potentially force them to close their doors.

A year before President Bush announced his national program, the U.S. Department of Labor's Center for Faith-Based and Community Initiatives designed a $25 million, three-year pilot program called Ready4Work to test various strategies. The agency's faith-based director, Brent Orrell, collaborated with Public Private Ventures (PPV), prisoner reentry practitioners, scholars, and philanthropists to build Ready4Work so it could overcome the obstacles and build upon the research findings that ex-prisoners who find and keep steady jobs and get connected in their communities have a much better chance of staying out of jail.

Operating with faith-based partnerships in eleven cities, Ready4Work targeted those most likely to return to prison—eighteen- to thirty-four-year-old, nonviolent, nonsexual offenders.

---

[64] http://www.cnn.com/2004/ALLPOLITICS/01/20/sotu.transcript.7/index.html

Across the country, the 4,500 ex-prisoners in the program were predominately black men, with an average age of twenty-six. Half had been arrested five or more times, and the majority had spent more than two years in prison.

With employment rates for ex-prisoners dismally low, the Ready4Work sites worked hard to provide job training for felons and nurture relationships with potential employers. Their work paid off, and almost 60 percent of Ready4Work participants got a job.[65]

Mentors Make the Difference

Men and women leaving prison needed accountable and supportive relationships to work around their cultural deficit. Reentry can be a time filled with so much fear, anger, isolation, confusion, and sadness that it can send ex-prisoners spiraling back down unless someone is there for them. Mentors supply both emotional and practical support. The practical support is necessary to meet the dozens of everyday challenges that years in prison can make so daunting, such as finding a place to live, getting a driver's license, and figuring out how to commute to work.

For twenty-five years, Gary Walker of Public Private Ventures (PPV) has been designing, developing, and evaluating many of the nation's leading initiatives for at-risk youth. "Faith-based programs are rooted in building strong adult-youth relationships and are less concerned with training, schooling, and providing services, which don't have the same direct impact on individual behavior.... [Only mentors can say], 'You need to change your life, I'm here to help you do it, or you need to be put away.'"[66] PPV evaluated the

[65] *Ready4Work: Final Research Report,* U.S. Department of Labor, September 2008.
[66] http://www.manhattan-institute.org/pdf/coh1.pdf.

mentoring component specifically and found that those who met with a mentor were twice as likely to obtain a job and stay in that job longer.

Ready4Work partners with churches to cultivate mentors. Mentors range in age from eighteen to eighty; most are male; and more than 85 percent are African American. The last point is significant. Traditional mentoring programs have often found it difficult to recruit a diverse body of volunteers, but a heroic network of African American pastors have called parishioners into action.

James from Jacksonville, Florida, is a wonderful example of the power of a mentor. James had a ten-year criminal history by the age of twenty-eight. Thanks to the support he received from Operation New Hope, a church mentoring program that works in tandem with Ready4Work, he has been employed for more than two-and-a-half years and is earning $11.25 per hour. He also has worked hard to repair his credit and was able to purchase a new home. Now he is giving back by return visits to Operation New Hope, where he shares his success in the Ready4Work program with others.

In his book, *Giving*, former President Bill Clinton lauded Operation New Hope and its founder, Rev. Kevin Gay, for its Ready4Work model.[67] As a presidential candidate, U.S. Senator Barack Obama also singled out Ready4Work as an example of the type of innovation he would pursue in his White House faith-based effort.

Scaling Prison Reform

When President Bush announced turning the trailblazing Ready4Work initiative into his full-scale Prisoner Reentry Initiative during the 2004 State of the Union Address, Julio Medina from New York City was seated next to First Lady Laura Bush. As founder of Exodus Transitional

---

[67] Bill Clinton, *Giving* (New York: Knopf, 2007).

Community (ETC), he has helped more than 3,000 men and women make the transition from prison to society. His own prison experience made him see that most of his fellow inmates did not want to continue a life of crime, but rather they simply wanted to be good citizens and heal some of the damage they had done.

However, when they got outside the prison walls and ran into barriers, they fell back into old patterns. He created ETC to help them overcome these obstacles, and he returns to prison regularly to deliver a message of hope. He also teaches at the New York Theological Seminary at the Sing Sing Correctional Facility in Auburn, New York.[68]

At a White House Compassion in Action roundtable I hosted on prisoner reentry initiatives, Medina introduced us to Greg, a young man who was profiled in the documentary *Hard Road Home*,[69] which highlights Medina's East Harlem Ready4Work site. Greg was first incarcerated as a juvenile, and then a second time as a young adult where he spent two years in prison. When he arrived at Medina's Ready4Work program, it was obvious that he was a kid who had made some serious mistakes, but he also showed intelligence, humor, warmth, and tremendous potential. Greg thrived in Medina's program. At the premier of *Hard Road Home*, he stood in front of a nearly full, 1,200-seat theater and explained that his journey was not over. "I'm still getting services from Exodus," he said, "so I can improve my skills and get a better job."

Ready4Work has served nearly 5,000 incarcerated individuals like James in Jacksonville and Greg in East Harlem. On average, the program costs approximately $4,500 per participant, which is far less than the $25,000 to $40,000 cost per year to house an inmate. Most important, Ready4Work re-arrest rates are

---

[68] http://www.etcny.org/Julio_Medina.html.

[69] *Hard Road Home*, Macky Alston and Andrea Meller, directors; Greenhouse Pictures, 2007.

44 percent lower than the national average, and despair has been replaced with hope.

By the time President Bush arrived in Baltimore to visit the Jericho Project in January 2008, the Departments of Justice (DOJ) and Labor (DOL) had implemented a new way of doing business, both inside the prison walls and post-release. DOJ was working with faith-based and community groups to prepare inmates for release, much like InnerChange, which had proven so successful in Texas. DOL built on its Ready4Work experience to partner with programs like Jericho to integrate these men and women back into society through good jobs and stable housing.

Between the DOJ and the DOL, there were thirty reentry programs being funded across the country, serving more than 10,000 ex-offenders. The vast majority of them were placed in jobs, and their re-arrest rate one year after release was less than half the national average. With final adoption of the Second Chance Act in 2008, the Bush era prisoner reentry reforms are now the new normal in criminal justice.[70]

"And How Are the Children?"

Mentors are the key to keeping ex-convicts from re-offending, but mentors are also critical for keeping the children of former felons from pursuing the same path. Children of prisoners are more likely to face material and familial instability than their peers. And in America today, there are more than 1.7 million minors who have one or both parents in some form of state or federal criminal supervision.[71] As the national press continued to cover the faith-based initiative merely as a debate in church-state relations,

---

[70] United States Department of Justice.

[71] "Parents in Prison and their Minor Children," Bureau of Justice Statistics (2010).

President Bush rallied the faith community to volunteer its time and invest its love in these at-risk youth. U.S. Department of Health and Human Services Center for Faith-Based and Community Initiatives director Bobby Polito collaborated with HHS Assistant Secretary Wade Horn to invest $49 million per year in the national Mentoring Children of Prisoners initiative. The program paired more than 100,000 children of prisoners with volunteer mentors from 2003 to 2008. To comprehend the enormity of this accomplishment, note that it took the esteemed Big Brothers Big Sisters *100 years* to find mentor matches for 100,000 children.

Much like InnerChange was the grassroots, faith-based inspiration behind the Prisoner Reentry program, President Bush's first faith-based director, John DiIulio, found the blueprints for President Bush's eventual Mentoring Children of Prisoners initiative in a Big Brothers Big Sisters/Public Private Partners venture called Amachi.[72] Led by the former mayor of Philadelphia, Reverend Wilson Goode, Amachi matches loving, faith-motivated mentors with at-risk children. They recruit mentors from the same neighborhoods where the kids live, which helps create a stronger community connection. Mentors are inspired by the program's mission, which is captured in its name. "Amachi" is a Nigerian Ibo word meaning "Who knows but what God has brought us through this child." The mentors help answer to that question in many positive ways.

Rev. Goode invokes another African saying to recruit mentors. He explains that the Masai warriors greet one another each morning with the phrase "Casserian Engeri." Translated, this means "And how are the children?" Warriors always give the traditional answer,

---

[72] http://www.amachimentoring.org.

"All the children are well," whether they are fathers or not. This priority of protecting the young and powerless meant that their community was safe and at peace. It's a question Goode challenges Americans to adopt, and it's a promise that the Mentoring Children of Prisoners initiative helped fulfill.

Consider the story of Kayla Booze, an angry teenager in New Orleans at risk of dropping out of school. Kayla had been an eager elementary student who got As in her classes and loved art projects before her father was arrested for shooting a man in a barbershop fight. Entering middle school lost in a haze of confusion and frustration over her absent father, Kayla was paired with Brenda Williams through the Mentoring Children of Prisoners program. Williams met with Kayla every two weeks. The two would go to church and out for meals, or they'd simply go for a walk in the park. Williams even joined Kayla's mom for a meeting with the principal to discuss Kayla's declining grades. Together, both mom and mentor sprung into action, and Kayla restored her grades, taught herself piano, and began preparing for college.[73]

The Obama administration ended the Mentoring Children of Prisoners program in 2012 despite the best efforts of Miss America 2012, Laura Kaeppler, who used her crown to lobby for the Domestic Policy Council to restore the funding. The Kenosha, Wisconsin, native had watched her own father taken to prison for a white-collar crime, and she credits a family friend for being her mentor during the crisis. "After dance class, she would do something as small as take me to McDonald's for a fifty-cent ice-cream cone and sit there in the parking lot and talk," Kaeppler said. "Had I not had Katie's guidance, it would have been very

---

[73] http://www.csmonitor.com/The-Culture/Family/2012/0325/No-child-left-alone-Volunteers-mentor-children-of-inmates.

easy to go down a negative path and follow a negative crowd of friends."[74]

One Heart

Undeterred by the federal government's diminished role, Big Brothers Big Sisters continues to expand its effort. In recent years, they've been teaming up with Texas high-school football to create a statewide mentoring initiative. The vision for the initiative grew out of a football game that showed how sports can be used to change lives.

To the casual fan, the last game of the season between Gainesville State School and Grapevine Faith Christian School appeared like any other prep school contest. The two teams from north of Dallas squared off under the Friday Night Lights; the band played, the popcorn popped, and the crowd cheered. But the color scheme was somehow out of place.

The Grapevine Faith Lions were donned in their red "home" jerseys. Their fans wore red coats, hats, and sweaters to brave the October North Texas chill. The opposing Gainesville State Tornadoes wore their white "away" team jerseys. So why had all those red-clad Lions fans formed a forty-yard cheer tunnel with a banner that said "Go Tornadoes" to welcome the opponents onto the field? And why had some 200 Lions fans filled the Tornadoes sideline bleachers to cheer for the visiting players by name?

Gainesville's quarterback and linebacker, Isaiah, was confused. He told sportswriter Rick Reilly, "I never in my life thought I'd hear people cheering for us to hit their kids, they wanted us to." In Riley's recounting of the story for ESPN, Riley quoted Isaiah's

---

[74] G. Jeffrey MacDonald, "Miss America has a faith-based platform for kids of prisoners," June 6, 2012, religionnews.com.

teammate Alex, who thought maybe the fans were confused. "They started yelling 'DEE-fense!' when their team had the ball. I said 'What? Why are they cheerin' for us?'"[75]

The Gainesville Tornadoes hadn't heard cheers in a long time, if ever. As a matter of fact, they are usually the recipients of jeers and snickers as they leave the field. Tornado lineman Gerald says, "We can tell people are a little afraid of us when we come to the games. You can see it in their eyes. They're lookin' at us like we're criminals."

The skeptical reaction is understandable. As their weekly opponents leave the field to hugs from classmates, a dozen uniformed officers line the Tornadoes for the ride back to their maximum-security facility, operated by the Texas Juvenile Justice Department.

There are no home games for these boys. Every game is on the road, and the only smiles they see through their face masks are for the other guys. That is, until they visited Grapevine.

When Gainesville appeared on the Lions schedule, head coach Kris Hogan had an idea. He emailed his team parents, asking them to help divide Lions' fans in two so half could cheer for the other team. Coach Hogan figured the Gainesville boys had probably never been cheered for at a game—he suspected they had more drug, robbery, and assault charges than touchdowns. His heart broke over the boys whose families had disowned them. "Here's the message I want you to send," Coach Hogan wrote to his team parents. "You're just as valuable as any other person on planet earth."

Reilly wrote that some of the Lions players were confused by the coach's game plan. Hogan replied, "Imagine you didn't have a home life. Imagine if everybody had pretty much given up on you.

---

[75] http://sports.espn.go.com/espnmag/story?id=3789373.

Now imagine what it would mean for hundreds of people to suddenly believe in you."

And that's just what happened when the Lions' parents and junior varsity cheerleading squad gave the Tornadoes their first-ever fans. The Grapevine players said that they could see hope fill the Tornadoes players' eyes. They hit with more intensity as the game went on, and they showered their coach with Gatorade bottles following their 33-14 *loss* to the Lions. After the game, Gainesville coach Mark Williams grabbed Coach Hogan by the shoulders and shouted, "You'll never know what your people did for these kids tonight. You'll never, ever know." Coach Williams later shared that most of his players are severely underdeveloped emotionally and socially. He said that their emotional maturity may have advanced three years during that ballgame.

This was evident the second the game clock ticked down to zero. When both teams assembled at midfield for prayer, Tornado quarterback Isaiah (Gainesville only releases first names) asked to lead the prayer. "Lord, I don't know how this happened, so I don't know how to say 'thank you,' but I never would've known there was so many people in the world that cared about us." Coach Hogan's tears gave testimony to the biblical admonition that it is better to give than receive.

Mentoring is about mutual transformation rather than one-way charity. Big Brothers Big Sisters CEO Charles Pierson is a former football player from Vanderbilt. He led the Texas Big Brothers Big Sisters operation before becoming CEO of the national office. On behalf of Big Brothers Big Sisters, Pierson is partnering with Steve Riach, producer of a new movie called *One Heart*, which will bring the Gainesville-Grapevine game to the silver screen.[76] Pierson

---

[76] *One Heart*, director Mark Robert Ellis; Et3rné Films, 2013.

hopes people will realize the power of sports and mentors in changing young people's lives. Pierson also is collaborating with Byron Johnson, a criminologist at Baylor University in Texas, to form the One Heart Texas Mentoring Initiative to reach 1,000 juvenile offenders each year for three years. Baylor will evaluate the program to determine its effects on social competence, academic improvements, and reduced recidivism.

There are 200,000 of America's youth incarcerated in juvenile facilities like Gainesville, and many are them are children of prisoners. The human services systems are often inadequate to handle the type of challenges these children face. Pierson, Riach, and Johnson know of a community asset that has the solution: local churches. The Big Brothers Big Sisters experience with Amachi, and now *One Heart,* paves the way for the faith community to save young lives.

Helping America's Youth

Another Texan, Laura Bush, has a similar heart for at-risk youth, which prompted her to make Helping America's Youth her signature initiative as First Lady. Announced by President Bush in the 2005 State of the Union, Helping America's Youth was a nationwide effort to raise awareness about the challenges facing youth, particularly at-risk boys like the ones at Gainesville, and to motivate caring adults to support youth in three key areas: family, school, and community.

Mrs. Bush began the effort by visiting exemplary programs, such as Homeboy Industries in Los Angeles. As his neighborhood achieved status as the gang capital of the world in the 1980s, Father Greg Boyle, or "Father G" to neighborhood kids, realized the only way to turn things around would be to work with gang members directly. Believing that "nothing stops a bullet like a job," he created an employment program for the gang members that eventually spun off new business start-ups, such as Homeboy Bakery, Homeboy Silkscreen, and Homeboy Graffiti Removal. Father G leveraged the kids' entrepreneurial talent and directed it in a constructive and profitable direction.

Mrs. Bush visited another gang violence prevention program in Chicago called CeaseFire, which sends former gang members to the streets as outreach workers. There they teach young people who've grown accustomed to violence what a better kind of cool looks like. The program's creator, Dr. Gary Slutkin, says that the former gangbangers are "followed around like Pied Pipers because these kids are so hungry for a good example."[77]

A different type of organization that made a deep impression on the First Lady was the National Debate Project in Atlanta, which uses debate techniques to improve the critical thinking and leadership skills of K–12 students from low-income neighborhoods. It also teaches them to resolve conflicts with their minds rather than their fists. Students participating in the program debated such topics as whether the United States should intervene in Sudan and whether rap music should be allowed in schools.

These visits led to a White House Conference on Helping America's Youth held at Howard University in October 2005. Mrs. Bush assembled more than 500 parents, civic leaders, faith-based groups, and experts to assess the problem and design solutions. Research was presented demonstrating the unique challenges that America's youth face today. Said Mrs. Bush:

"We all know that the challenges facing young people in the United States today are far greater than they were for

---

[77] Dr. Gary Slutkin quoted in Laura Bush speech at Regional Conference on Helping America's Youth, November 8, 2007.

children just a generation ago. Drugs and gangs, predators on the Internet, violence on television and in real life are just some of the negative influences that are present everywhere today. And as children face these challenges, they often have fewer people to turn to for help. More children are raised in single-parent families, most often without a father. Millions of children have one or both of their parents in prison. Many boys and girls spend more time alone or with their peers than they do with any member of their family."[78]

Following this White House conference, the First Lady hosted six regional conferences—Indiana, Colorado, Tennessee, Minnesota, Texas, and Oregon—and she participated in 125 other events in twenty-four states, plus the District of Columbia, to train local youth-serving organizations. One tool that proved especially useful was the Web-based *Community Guide to Helping America's Youth*. This guide highlights resources Americans can use to form partnerships and implement successful programs.

To ensure the continuity of Mrs. Bush's youth initiative, the president signed an executive order to establish an Interagency Working Group on Youth Programs to continue the coordination of faith-based programs with the federal government that Helping America's Youth had created. It also tasked the work group with developing rigorous program assessments to determine best practices and promote cost effective solutions for achieving better results for at-risk youth, such as mentoring.

In his 2003 State of the Union address, President Bush said, "One mentor, one person, can change a life forever." Through

---

[78] Laura Bush speech at Regional Conference on Helping America's Youth, November 8, 2007.

a combination of Mentoring Children of Prisoners, Helping America's Youth, and other Bush administration compassion agenda efforts to combat youth violence and build healthy life skills in all children, the Bushes demonstrated their love for children. They also used their White House platform to show that government can help place problems before the public, but it is only the heroic work of community partners who can solve them.

Modern-Day Abolitionists

Criminals aren't the only prisoners who need to be set free. There are 27 million people who live in modern-day slavery around the world, a total greater than all those taken from Africa in the 400-year trans-Atlantic slave trade. Human sex trafficking is a $32 billion annual industry, making it the third largest industry of illicit activity on the planet, with profits greater than ExxonMobil.

Like William Wilberforce, who, more than 200 years ago, leaned on people of faith to help end slavery across the British Empire, today's faith community plays a central role in both combating human trafficking and helping its victims heal. International Justice Mission (IJM) founder Gary Haugen leads a team of 300 full-time lawyers, criminal investigators, and social workers mobilized in sixteen offices around the world. Motivated by faith and equipped by their professional training, the IJM staff conducts professional investigations, intervenes on behalf of the victims, holds perpetrators accountable, and seeks structural change.

President Bush hosted the first national training conference on combating human trafficking in Tampa, Florida, in July 2004. Calling trafficking a new form of slavery, Bush noted the seriousness of the problem: Each year, an estimated 600,000 to 800,000 men, women, and children are trafficked against their will across international borders; 14,500 to 17,500 of whom are trafficked into the United States. Victims of trafficking are recruited, transported, or sold into all forms of forced labor and servitude, including prostitution, sweatshops, domestic labor, farming, and child armies. Approximately 80 percent of trafficking victims are female, and 70 percent of those female victims are trafficked for the commercial sex industry.[79]

> "Human trafficking is an offense against human dignity, a crime in which human beings, many of them teenagers and young children, are bought and sold and often sexually abused by violent criminals... No one is fit to be a master and no one deserves to be a slave.... Our nation is determined to fight and end this modern form of slavery."
> —George W. Bush[80]

When George W. Bush took office, very few people outside the International human rights community had ever even heard of the term human trafficking. In his first term, Bush spent $295 million to combat trafficking in 120 countries. This funding was used to create special law enforcement units for this specialized crime and to care for victims, including $35 million to faith-based groups to providing healing. In 2004, the State Department began elevating the profile of this issue with the release of its annual Trafficking in

---

[79] George W. Bush, speech at the National Training Conference on Human Trafficking, July 16, 2004.
[80] George W. Bush at the signing of the H.R. 972, Trafficking Victims Protection Reauthorization Act.

Persons report, which includes data on the scope of the problem and analysis of 140 countries' efforts to combat it. Countries that are the worst offenders are now exposed and threatened with sanctions.[81]

At a White House Compassion in Action roundtable in 2007, IJM's Gary Haugen told a story about a Cambodian woman named Mary and her daughter, Bofa, who lived in a squatter camp outside Kampong Chnang. One day some men came to the family and told them they could get Bofa a job peeling shrimp in the port cities. Mary refused, but the predators prevailed on Bofa's sense of financial responsibility for her family and wooed her away without allowing her to tell her mother. Mary thought Bofa was dead, but then she heard news from a friend that the girl was seen across the border locked in a Thai brothel.

The people who offered Bofa the job peeling shrimp were actually sex traffickers who beat her into submission and sold her repeatedly to paying customers. Mary called the police, but they demanded money. Unbeknownst to her, the U.S. government had funded IJM to train a police unit in Cambodia to fight sex trafficking. IJM rescued Bofa, as well as nine other women and children abducted by the same trafficking ring, and then they assisted in the brothel keepers' arrests.

My Sagamore Institute colleague, Amy Sherman, serves as a senior advisor to Haugen. They are considering ways to enlarge the role of the local church in this effort. IJM is able to get thousands of girls out of brothels, but it is only the transforming work of the church that can get the brothel out of the girl. Dr. Beth Grant,

---

[81] George W. Bush, speech at the National Training Conference on Human Trafficking, July 16, 2004.

who, with her husband, formed Homes of Hope, a safe house for trafficked girls, told our White House roundtable gathering how this can be done.

Ten years ago, Grant received a call from her colleague in Bombay, who discovered more than 100 women enslaved at the brothels. "Can you please take thirty-seven little girls?" her colleague pleaded with her. Grant and her husband said "yes" and formed Homes of Hope, which now sponsors eleven aftercare homes in India and Nepal. They were stunned to learn that they are fighting a problem that has existed for thousands of years, since girls were trafficked through this region into the courts of ancient kings.

Grant has translated her program's success into a curriculum for the Faith Alliance against Slavery and Trafficking. Called "Hands That Heal," Grant teaches how to minister to the whole person. "What strikes me when I look into the eyes of victims in Calcutta, or Mumbai, or wherever I meet them, is the death in their eyes," says Grant. To deal with the horror of their experience, something had to die in order for them to survive. Healing that wound must be transformational, and it must be holistic. "We believe that only God can take the brothel out of a young woman's mind, body, and spirit and change the way she sees herself, so that she realizes she was created for a purpose and *that* is not it."

Serious challenges remain. The need is the same in America as in other nations: to improve victim identification, rescue, police training, sensitizing judges, and other complexities. Perhaps the biggest problem is the insidious nature of the crime itself. While much has changed since the days of the trans-Atlantic slave trade, the lie which fueled that horrific chapter in history—a belief that some people are less than human—is at the root of sex trafficking and slave labor today. Their subsequent demeaning actions are so violent and noxious that victims are afraid of being considered dirty, or criminals, or illegal aliens. Yet, we can't help them until we find them. Again, grassroots, faith-based healers prove indispensible allies in such a labyrinthine task.

Legislation and the Ongoing Campaign

President George Bush signed the William Wilberforce Trafficking Victims Protection Reauthorization Act of 2008 just before leaving office. He had worked with Congress on several similar pieces of legislation throughout his administration, but his final act was named for legislator from England who, as a youth, listened to Parliament debate the American Revolution.

Wilberforce has been the inspiration for many abolition-ists since his work in ending the British slave trade, including a fifteen-year-old from Atlanta named Zach Hunter. As Zach read about the history of oppression in America, he became angry at the injustice and dreamed of working alongside Frederick Douglas to end what Condoleezza Rice calls "America's birth defect." He then discovered how human trafficking had become a modern form of slavery, and he immediately found a cause fitting his generation.

Zach started the Loose Change to Loosen Chains campaign to raise funds and awareness. In the first eighteen months of his outreach, he spoke to a half-million students about the problem and the problem-solvers. "I believe God wants to use my generation to do great things and to improve the world," said Hunter. "I've told them (the students) something that Gary Haugen has taught me: that God has a plan to end the suffering and injustice in the world and his plan is us."

We invited Zach to speak at our White House Compassion in Action roundtable event alongside Haugen. He told us how his generation might be perceived as self-centered, but they know that the world is a small place because the media lets us see the suffering up close, and many of them feel responsible for what's going on. As we closed the roundtable with a video tribute to Wilberforce commemorating the 200th anniversary of his actions, Zach rolled out a petition across the President's Eisenhower Executive Office Building briefing room stage featuring more than 100,000 signatures of students and leaders who want to see slavery end. The campaign against injustice continues.

Mrs. Bush launched a campaign of her own on November 17, 2001, when she became the first woman to deliver a presidential weekly radio address. She used the occasion to speak out against the Taliban's harsh treatment of women and children and to launch her public advocacy on behalf of the women of Afghanistan in the immediate aftermath of 9/11.

The First Lady put her ideas into action by helping to develop and lead the U.S.–Afghan Women's Council and by delivering remarks to gatherings such as the International Conference (*Centre de Conferences Internationals*) in support of the people of Afghanistan. In 2001, fewer than a million Afghan children were in school, and all of them were boys. At the end of the Bush presidency, six million Afghan children were attending school, and one-third of them were girls.[82]

Mrs. Bush has a well-earned reputation of being graceful and soft-spoken. An exception to the soft-spoken part was on display over the human rights violations in Burma. She became

---

[82] *Progress toward Security and Stability in Afghanistan*, Report to Congress, January, 2009, 72.

an outspoken critic of the military junta and a vocal advocate for jailed opposition leader Aung San Suu Kyi. In an opinion piece in the *Wall Street Journal*[83] bemoaning the fact that Suu Kyi spent her sixty-second birthday under house arrest and in joining sixteen female U.S. senators in signing a letter urging the United Nations to step up pressure on the Burmese regime to release the political prisoner, she made sure her voice was heard.

Domestic Violence

Much like human trafficking, domestic violence flourishes in the dark corners of communities, where only caring neighbors can detect it. The issue of domestic violence has been in the public conscience for much longer than human trafficking, but it is kept neatly out of public view. Those who have stepped into this gap are highly motivated and sorely under-resourced. That prompted the Justice Department Center on Faith-Based and Community Initiatives to work with agency staff to offer grants and training on such topics such as listening to and working with abused women, domestic violence in rural settings, and safety planning.

The Justice Department's Office of Violence Against Women supplied a $2.9 million grant to thirty-nine rural, faith-based, and community organizations nationwide. Sandra Renfrow, director of a rural domestic violence shelter in southwest Arkansas, was one recipient of a Faith and Community Technical Support (FACTS) grant. At a FACTS event my office hosted at Baylor University (which administered the program), Renfrow told a story of a woman who was taken hostage from her Colorado home by a "boyfriend," who was a truck driver. Beaten and raped along their route south,

---

[83] "Bush: Suu Kyi's Long Journey to Freedom," *Wall Street Journal*, September 18, 2012.

she was allowed to use a public restroom in Arkansas. It was there that she saw a flyer for Renfrow's organization and tore off the telephone number.

The woman was able to escape in the next town. She found a police officer and showed him the domestic violence shelter information. Renfrow received a midnight call saying the woman was in an emergency room sixty miles away and wanted her help. Renfrow explained that she used grant funding for a "mobile outreach program" including posting flyers with phone numbers on little tear-off slips in every public women's restroom across six Arkansas counties. Within a couple of months, they saw their call volume double and a 62 percent increase in shelter use. Grassroots groups do not require a lot of money to have an outsized impact.

A woman named Kim from my home state of Indiana had been a victim of abuse for years. She lived in a remote part of the state, and her perpetrator would continuously taunt her by saying, "Nobody can help you here." She believed him, and the suffering persisted until one of our FACTS grassroots partners rescued her. Someone did find her, and rescued her, thanks to this project.

The return on investment for FACTS grants was impressive. The thirty-nine grantees increased services by 200 percent in such ways as help with down payments, job readiness, legal aid, and transportation. FACTS also translated into a staggering increase in volunteers and community education programs. Because of the overall success of this program, local centers that received FACTS grants were awarded another $1.5 million in non-federal grants and donations after the FACTS grants ended.

Human trafficking and domestic violence are two examples of violence against women both at home and abroad. The return of prisoners to society and the prevention of at-risk teens from becoming incarcerated themselves are among the nation's important justice pursuits. Through the compassionate response of caring individuals and the resources provided by the government, solutions are rising.

4

FAITH IN THE STATES

The story of how governors embraced and expanded the faith-based initiative is as remarkable as it was ignored by the national media. The governors who rallied to President Bush's faith-based vision filled the Democratic and Republic primaries in both 2008 and 2012. Names such as Bill Richardson, Jeb Bush, Sarah Palin, Tim Pawlenty, Janet Napolitano, Bob McDonnell, and Mitch Daniels represented the true laboratories of democracy. They set up their offices in different ways, took on different priorities, and made progress at varying speeds. But they all recognized that the real work was done by neighborhood healers and social entrepreneurs, so they did their best to fuel grassroots enterprises.

There were a total of thirty-five governors who implemented a faith-based office similar to the Bush model, and more than half of them were Democrats. Also, a dozen governors left office after starting a faith-based office, and in every instance their successor retained the office, regardless of party affiliation.

Our local strategy went not only to state capitols but to the territories of Puerto Rico and Guam as well. Governors Luis Fortuno and Felix Comacho were both ardent supporters of faith-based strategies, and each participated at White House conferences, telling of the positive difference these groups made in their homeland.

In advancing the initiative we were also joined by over 100 mayors across the country. U.S. Conference of Mayors President and Miami Mayor Manny Diaz was particularly active through the President's $1.5 million Compassion Capital Fund grant, which supported a collaboration between his office and local nonprofits aimed at serving Miami's neighbors in need. In addition to capacity building services (fundraising, board development, and outcomes measurement), the coalition redistributed most of the funding to the grassroots groups serving at-risk children, prisoners reentering the region, and adults preparing for marriage and transitioning from welfare to work.

In this chapter, we'll look at how individual states have carried the banner for the faith-based movement in effective and economically efficient ways. By highlighting initiatives in various states, I hope you'll gain a sense for what can be accomplished when citizen activism is paired with state partnership.

Alaska

Sarah Palin provides a useful study of contrasts. On the national stage, her firebrand style of politics rallies faith and values voters with stump speeches appealing to Tea Party and Religious Right themes of family, faith, and flag; indeed, her second book used those exact terms in its subtitle. When talking of her personal faith, Palin is warm and authentic.

That is the Sarah Palin I met in 2008, one year prior to being discovered by the McCain campaign. Alaska's relatively unknown governor invited me to keynote her annual faith-based and volunteerism conference. My office had a standing policy of saying "yes" to all gubernatorial requests as part of our desire to shift attention away from Capitol Hill to the states where compassion is delivered more than it is debated.

Soon after confirming my participation in Alaska, the White House scheduled the South Lawn ceremony honoring my home-town Indianapolis Colts' Super Bowl victory on the very same date. After an internal debate about whether I should cancel the trip because Colts Coach Tony Dungy is a friend of mine and an ally of the faith-based initiative, I knew the right place to be was Anchorage.

Alaska had become an ideal example of how states not only rally the armies of compassion but how they are uniquely positioned to serve these hometown heroes. Governor Palin formed a faith-based council chaired by Scott Merriner, a Harvard- and Oxford-educated pastor from one of Anchorage's largest churches. He returned to his native Alaska from a McKinsey & Co. management consultant job in South Africa to serve as the founding director of Grace Alaska, a nonprofit arm of the church that featured car repairs for low-income families, a soup kitchen, backpacks for the homeless, and other services.

Sometimes called "The Last Frontier" because of its many sparsely populated villages, Alaska is a state of magnificent beauty and too often unspeakable human problems. A survey reveals that more than half of the women in the state are victims of domestic violence, a problem magnified by its remoteness and desperation faced by men unable to maintain their hunting and fishing liveli-hoods.[84] These are the type of problems that must be addressed at village-level by highly engaged nonprofits. Governor Palin and her successor Sean Parnell operated a Compassion Capital Fund grant

---

[84] http://justice.uaa.alaska.edu/avs.

program that strengthened such grassroots groups in seven Alaska communities.

Arizona

Arizona Governor Janet Napolitano was a prominent Democrat who impressively formed and led her state's faith-based initiative. As her state's attorney general before becoming governor, she took seriously the constitutional parameters of church-state relations, and therefore she was one of the nation's most credible proponents of the Bush administration model.

Governor Napolitano served as the chairperson of the National Governor's Association during 2007, and her vice chair was Minnesota Governor Tim Pawlenty. I designed a series of White House conferences to highlight state innovation, and I began with these two states because of each governor's impressive leadership and innovation, as well as to signal the bipartisan nature of the initiative.

The Lodestar Center for Philanthropy and Nonprofit Innovation at Arizona State University produced a comprehensive report recognizing the state's status as the first to play host to this new series. The report quoted Governor Napolitano explaining the "why" behind her formation of the faith-based office's efforts: "[to promote] the ways in which Arizona has embraced its sacred and secular nonprofits as an integral part of the fabric of local communities... [and to build] our human infrastructure—the network of people and organizations who restore the lives of those who are poor and most vulnerable."[85]

---

[85] "ASU Center for Nonprofit Leadership and Management collaborates with Governor's office to produce faith and community initiatives publication"; Arizona State University Press Release, November 16, 2007.

On the eve of the conference, then-Governor Napolitano and I co-hosted a private showing of *Amazing Grace*, a film about British abolitionist William Wilberforce, whose life exemplified the themes we would address in the conference. Lodestar researchers presented the Pima County One-Stop system as a success story for the Arizona faith-based initiative. In 2004, the One-Stop received a special capacity-building grant from the U.S. Department of Labor (DOL) to develop faith-based and grassroots access points for workforce-related service delivery to hard-to-reach populations: ex-offenders, people with limited English proficiency, homeless individuals, high-school dropouts, people with drug or alcohol addiction, welfare recipients, and children aging out of foster care. At the end of three years, this network provided mentoring and job training for 412 people and helped 217 successfully enter the job market.[86]

Minnesota

The Minnesota Conference was next, but my plans to meet with Governor Pawlenty for a pre-event strategy session were cast aside when my boss arrived in town that day to survey the damage of the tragic I-35 bridge collapse. On August 1, 2007, the eight-lane steel truss arch bridge crossing the Mississippi River in Minneapolis collapsed during rush hour. President and Mrs Bush arrived in the Twin Cities to discuss the federal government's assistance with recovery and rebuilding and to comfort the mourning and injured. President Bush also met with the volunteers who were selfless and heroic in the immediate aftermath.

---

[86] *Restoring Lives, Transforming Communities: Building a Strong Foundation through Faith and Community Initiatives*, The Lodestar Center for Philanthropy and Nonprofit Innovation at Arizona State University, 2007.

One of those heroes was Matthew Miller, a twenty-two-year-old student at nearby Bethel University who was doing summer construction work to resurface the bridge when it collapsed. Miller risked his life to save eight injured people trapped in the part of the bridge that buckled. Jeremy Hernandez was another lifesaver. The twenty-year-old kicked open the emergency exit of a school bus carrying sixty-three children back home from a field trip to the water park. The school bus had slammed into a burning semitrailer and was hanging precariously against the guardrail of a broken part of the bridge. Hernandez ushered kids out of the bus and carried them to safety.

On August 5, while 1,400 people gathered for an interfaith healing service at St. Mark's Episcopal Cathedral, we honored the victims and rescuers of the Minnesota bridge tragedy at our White House conference. In my opening remarks, I called attention to the state's top-tier status in volunteerism. Minneapolis-St. Paul is the number one ranked metro area in the country, with 945,000 volunteers who served 106.7 million hours per year. Governor Pawlenty followed with his keynote address; he attributed those rankings to "Minnesota Nice," which is an apt moniker that depicts the thoughtfulness among its residents. In 2004, when the state faced a severe influenza vaccine shortage, many Minnesotans willingly gave up a flu shot so that others could take advantage of the medicine.

Not only is Minnesota a national pacesetter for volunteerism, the state also sends an inordinate number of National Guard troops overseas. When Pawlenty attends deployment ceremonies, he's humbled by the youthfulness and self-sacrifice of the servicemen and women. He says the only words that capture his emotions come from Isaiah 6:8—"Then I heard the voice of the Lord saying, 'Whom shall I send? And who will go for us?' And I said, 'Here am I. Send me!'"

"Through this catastrophe shines goodness. Goodness through first responders, emergency workers, fire and rescue workers, and everyday citizens. Instead of running away from danger, their first instinct was to run toward it to help others. We always talk about the Minnesota Nice. I don't think that goodness is detached from everything else. It's not goodness without a foundation. It's not goodness untethered from some principles or pillars. It's not goodness in a vacuum. I think goodness in my belief system comes from God, and I am not embarrassed to say that."

—Tim Pawlenty, Governor of Minnesota[87]

First Lady Mary Pawlenty launched the Beyond Yellow Ribbon campaign in 2003. For the thousands coming back from battle, the Yellow Ribbon initiative supports soldiers and their families with job placement and counseling, when needed, to help them reintegrate into society. In 2008, Congress established Minnesota's Yellow Ribbon Program as the national standard for all returning National Guard soldiers and their family members. Governor Pawlenty also created the Minnesota Family Covenant with the Secretary of the U.S. Army, promising that the state will "be there for military families when soldiers have to leave to fight."[88]

Mapping Out Change State by State

As we traveled from state to state, it was clear that some version of Minnesota Nice was on display in each place. However, it became

---

[87] White House Conference on Faith Based and Community Initiatives, Minnesota, August 9, 2007.
[88] The Minnesota Military Family and Community Covenant.

apparent to me that the media and too many others saw only the sentimentality in our mission rather than its sophistication. Not every governor was like Napolitano and Pawlenty. To put it bluntly, some governors thought the issue belonged on the First Lady's desk for ceremonial occasions rather than the governor's desk as part of the serious business of running the state.

My White House team—Diane Davis, Elizabeth Wiebe, Kristen Henderson, and Ivette Diaz—brainstormed solutions for raising awareness and advocacy for faith-based initiatives at the state level. Each state possessed a dynamic confluence of faith-based and community tools for fixing great human needs. However, they were often deployed in silos—virtually in secret, apart from public recognition. We needed an instrument to illustrate the collective action and summarize the big wins. We hit upon a simple but powerful tool: the map.

PRESIDENT BUSH'S FAITH-BASED AND COMMUNITY INITIATIVE ACTIVE IN ALL 50 STATES

★ Federal Grant Awards to State
Faith-Based and Community Organizations

☆ Federal Grant Awards to Support
Presidential FBCI Projects in All States

Idaho

One of my first attempts to roll this plan out was in Idaho. Against the backdrop of Matt Damon premiering his latest *Bourne Identity* film in downtown Boise, I joined Idaho Governor Butch Otter for remarks to the state's nonprofit leaders. Governor Otter had all the markings of a tough, Western leader. He wore cowboy boots and attributed his 1992 DUI charge to soaking his chewing tobacco in Jack Daniels. As he addressed the crowd, I could tell that his appreciation was sincere, but he definitely saw the nonprofits as more sweet than serious problem-solvers.

When it was my turn, I flashed the Idaho map on the screen and noticed the governor rise a little higher in his chair as he surveyed the icons scattered from border to border across the state. The headline-grabbing statistic for Governor Otter was that his state's nonprofits had won $117 million in federal grants the previous year with which to address problems such as job loss, drug addiction, homelessness, school dropouts, and much more.[89] This was not a mere goodwill gesture of altruism by volunteers who decided to tackle sentimental issues. This was real money—above and beyond his state's budget—awarded to Idaho because people of faith were creative and competitive in winning funding to solve problems that affect their communities.

Our map included "stars" placed on the Idaho communities that were implementing President Bush's signature faith-based initiatives, such as the Compassion Capital Fund (which built capacity for grassroots charities), the Mentoring Children of Prisoners initiative, and $22 million that funded hundreds of state drug treatment programs through Access to Recovery.

---

[89] *The President's Faith Based and Community Initiative in 50 States: A Report to the Nation.* The White House, June 2008.

Governor Otter was duly impressed by the reach of his non-profit community, and he began to barrage me with penetrating questions about the map. He wanted me to share the data with his state officials so that they could cross-tabulate the results by region. Clearly, they could avoid redundancy, leverage assets, and fill gaps by this type of evidence-based research. He not only took the bait, he was clearly seeing the business of nonprofits as a rich, value-added aspect of Idaho's magnificent landscape.

California

California's governor, Arnold Schwarzenegger, was part of the one-third of governors who did not open a faith-based office in his state. Word out of Sacramento was that the state didn't want to wade into the church–state quagmire. My office used the February 2008 National Governors Association meeting at the White House to help Governor Schwarzenegger, along with the other governors who had opted out of the faith-based movement, see how their states were still participating in faith-based initiatives regardless of their office's decision not to formally recognize these efforts. To make our case, we prepared a fifty-state report that President Bush delivered to the nation's governors who gathered at the White House in February 2008—a report depicting maps for every state (see California's example).

My team delighted in seeing Governor Schwarzenegger pick up his copy of the report and thumb through the pages until he located California. We watched as he read about the $1.1 billion his faith-based and community groups won in the previous year alone in their own determined attack on the Golden State's needs.[90]

---

[90] *The President's Faith Based and Community Initiative in 50 States: A Report to the Nation.* The White House, June 2008.

CALIFORNIA
FAITH-BASED AND COMMUNITY INITIATIVE ACTIVITIES

FEDERAL GRANT AWARDS TO CALIFORNIA FAITH-BASED AND COMMUNITY ORGANIZATIONS (2005–2006)***:

- Over $2.1 billion through 2,978 Federal grant awards
- $1,984,620,724 to secular nonprofits
- $205,854,700 to faith-based organizations

INCLUDED IN FEDERAL GRANTS TO CALIFORNIA ARE AWARDS TO FUND PRESIDENTIAL INITIATIVES***:

- Compassion Capital Fund (2002–2006): $12.4 million to nonprofits in 53 California cities
- Prisoner Reentry Initiative (2005–2006): $4.6 million to 7 nonprofits in 4 California cities
- Mentoring Children of Prisoners (2003–2007): $15 million to nonprofits in 21 California cities
- Access to Recovery (2004–2006): $22.8 million to California nonprofits

In 2006, 6.47 million California volunteers dedicated 858.5 million hours of service, according to the Corporation for National and Community Service *Volunteering in America 2007* report.

California's $1 Billion Solution

California presents a unique FBCI story because it lacks a gubernatorial-appointed office or liaison. For a casual observer of the initiative, that would suggest that the state is inactive. Yet, the state's faith-based and community sector is responding to the president's call for action and achieving impressive results.

In FY 2006, California nonprofits won 1,563 competitive federal awards. These awards brought nearly $1.1 billion to California to boost services to the needy.[91] During a time of restrained state resources for social services, leveraging federal competitive award dollars is especially meaningful.

Examples of California nonprofits advancing innovative public-private partnerships to solve stubborn social ills include:

- *The Prisoner Reentry Initiative (PRI):* Four California nonprofit sites won grants of $660,000 per year to provide post-release job training, mentoring, and other transition services to ex-prisoners. The California Department of Corrections has received grants to provide pre-release services in tandem with these sites. Nationwide, PRI participants recidivate at rates less than half the national average.
- *Access to Recovery (ATR):* $35 million in federal grants to the state of California and the California Rural Indian Health Board have enabled the creation of voucher-based addiction

---

[91] *The President's Faith Based and Community Initiative in 50 States: A Report to the Nation.* The White House, June 2008.

recovery programs. Through more than 400 nonprofit partners, ATR in California has provided clinical and/or support services to over 17,000 recovering addicts. ATR clients had a higher change in reduction of alcohol and drug use when compared to those receiving non-ATR services.

- *Mentoring Children of Prisoners (MCP):* MCP grants to California nonprofits have matched more than 3,000 caring mentors with children of incarcerated parents.
- *The Compassion Capitol Fund (CCF):* Since 2002, more than 100 nonprofits across fifty California cities have won grants—ranging from $50,000–$500,000—to expand their capabilities to serve the needy.
- Hundreds of other nonprofits have used federal funds to partner with federal, state, and local government to shelter homeless veterans, tutor students in struggling schools, provide job training, and serve their communities in a vast diversity of other ways.

Indiana's Blueprint

U.S. Senator Dan Coats of Indiana is considered by many to be the original compassionate conservative on Capitol Hill. With support from the likes of Jack Kemp and Bill Bennett, Coats authored the Project for American Renewal in 1995 to promote tax credits, restorative justice, and other private sector solutions to combat poverty. Many of these strategies would become key planks in President Bush's faith-based agenda five years later.

It was the enterprising Stephen Goldsmith, mayor of Indianapolis, who gave then-governor Bush a blueprint to consider for the eventual White House faith-based office. Goldsmith created the Front Porch Alliance, one of the nation's earliest government-led faith-based initiatives. Benefiting from the counsel of social entrepreneur Bob Woodson, Goldsmith didn't set up the pioneering model as a government funding program, or even a public sponsor of select projects. Rather, it was a civic switchboard, utilizing the power of City Hall to convene and connect resources to community needs.

For example, he took on the problem of drug deals in neglected city parks by engaging faith groups from the same neighborhoods to maintain them. It cost the city less, and the local presence pushed the drug dealers away and removed the graffiti from park buildings. The city formed 600 such partnerships during Goldsmith's tenure, some of them financial but most not. It was a simple formula of City Hall empowering indigenous leaders in place of the centralized approach taken by the 1960s Model Cities program that Goldsmith says supplanted neighborhood leadership.

Goldsmith was part of a crop of innovative mayors elected in the early 1990s that eschewed wealth distribution and the trumpeting of the city's pathologies to seek more federal aid in favor of new ideas to make their cities work better for all citizens. New York's Rudy Giuliani and Chicago's Richard Daley were among those who believed mayors should be "custodians not controllers of the public square," to quote Goldsmith.

My former Hudson Institute colleague Ryan Streeter collaborated with Goldsmith on a book called *Putting Faith in Neighborhoods*,[92] which detailed this new model of municipal citizenship. In his later role as professor at Harvard's Kennedy School of Government, Goldsmith published a paper called "City Hall and Religion: When, Why and How to Lead,"[93] in which he states that there is nothing new to faith-based groups providing

---

[92] Stephen Goldsmith and Ryan Streeter, *Putting Faith in Neighborhoods: Making Cities Work through Grassroots Citizenship* (Washington, DC: Hudson Institute, 2002).

[93] http://www.urbanministry.org/files/city-hall-and-religion.pdf.

social welfare services in U.S. cities and claimed that they were a useful remedy to government's neglect or simply a case of need outpacing supply.

He then examines several big city mayors who similarly advanced faith-based strategies: Patrick McCrory of Charlotte, North Carolina; Glenda Hood of Orlando, Florida; William Purcell of Nashville, Tennessee; Martin O'Malley of Baltimore, Maryland; Graham Richard of Fort Wayne, Indiana; R.T. Rybak of Minneapolis, Minnesota; and Anthony Williams of Washington, D.C. These mayors were diverse in their politics, race, and geography, but they each viewed faith as a common good.

Such pragmatism is the hallmark of state and local officials. It was the governors who finally ended twenty years of welfare debate, often marked by name calling in Washington, by actually reforming the system from the bottom up. Similarly, it was the government officials closest to the people who understood that faith-based social services were necessary to complete the work of welfare reform. Life change happens in grassroots ministries more than in government programs. For governors and mayors, success is measured not by legislation passed, but by action taken.

On November 5, 2008, I was joined at a White House conference in Indianapolis by two Hoosier leaders who knew how to put faith into action, Mitch Daniels and Tony Dungy. Daniels helped establish a faith-based K–8 school called The Oaks Academy while serving as a business executive with Eli Lilly & Co. The school, located in one of Indianapolis' struggling neighborhoods, offers a classical education model that attracts talented kids from both suburban and inner city families.

As Indiana governor, Daniels was one of the first state executives to launch a faith-based office in tandem with the state's administration of federal volunteer programs. This is actually quite common sense but rare compared to Washington and most states that tend to put government programs in silos. Daniels' combined effort contributed to Indiana's success in bolstering 1.25 million Hoosier volunteers who contributed over 242 million hours of service every year.[94]

The media was impressed that Indianapolis Colts Head Coach Tony Dungy joined Daniels in helping me kick off the White House conference the day after his team lost a high profile game against their rival, the New England Patriots. Dungy quickly assured them that he considered our event to be equally important. For him, community service and loving one's neighbor as oneself was what he expected among his players inside the locker room—and of himself outside of it.

Daniels and Dungy were joined at the conference by Jim Morris, a longtime Indianapolis civic leader, who was at that time serving as executive director of the United Nations World Food Program. He focused his remarks on the Indiana imprint on the Bush administration's revolutionary effort to combat AIDS in Africa detailed in Chapter 5.

Also reflecting Indiana's global faith-based footprint was White House conference speaker Marta Gabre-Tsadick, who was the first woman senator to serve in the Ethiopian government. Fearing execution during a Communist takeover in 1974, she and her husband fled to Fort Wayne, Indiana, where she was given sanctuary by a church and was joined by partners there to form a relief organization called Project Mercy. With offices in Fort Wayne and Yetebon, Ethiopia, Project Mercy includes a hospital, school,

---

[94] *Volunteering in America: 2007 State Trends and Rankings.* Corporation for National and Community Service, 2007.

and orphanage and offers microloans, agriculture innovations, and community development solutions. Her riveting story is told in the book *Sheltered by the King*.[95]

Planted in both Indiana and Ethiopian soil, Gabre-Tsadick's ministry demonstrates that the faith-based initiative was global long before it was prominent in national policy. The next chapter takes a much closer look at the U.S.–Africa faith and service partnership.

---

[95] Marga Gabre-Tsadick, *Sheltered by the King* (Grand Rapids: Zondervan, 1983).

5

TO WHOM MUCH IS GIVEN ...
HELPING AFRICA HEAL

"To whom much is given, much is required." This simple but powerful biblical precept is the answer George W. Bush gives when asked why an American president would create the largest international health initiative dedicated to a single disease in the history of the world.

Between 1999 and 2000, more people died of AIDS in Africa than in all the previous wars on the continent. The year 2000 began with 24 million Africans infected with the virus plus 11,000 new infections and 6,000 deaths mounting every day. With one in ten schoolteachers expected to die within five years, this was not only human tragedy but a crisis that put the whole continent at risk. Experts concluded that without a medical miracle, more than 20 million AIDS sufferers would be dead by 2010.[96]

The miracle came from the United States after an unlikely alliance formed between a compassionate conservative president, an Irish rock star, an irascible chairman of the Senate Foreign Relations Committee (well-known for his opposition to foreign aid), and an evangelist from the Blue Ridge Mountains. The list

---

[96] Lester R. Brown, "HIV Epidemic Restructuring Africa's Population," *World Watch Issue Alert*, 31 October 2000.

of things that separated George Bush, Bono, Jesse Helms, and Franklin Graham would be impressive in length and variety. Yet, these men shared a Christian faith, a belief that the world cannot watch a generation of Africans perish from disease, and the will do something about it.

Think Big

Africa needed a game-changer, and that is exactly what President Bush ordered Secretary of State Colin Powell and Secretary of Health and Human Services Tommy Thompson to create. They were ably served by Dr. Anthony Fauci, a longtime infectious disease director at the National Institutes for Health, whose expertise and diligence would largely shape the U.S. strategy.

The first step in Fauci's plan was to stop the disease's rapid escalation. Without any intervention, up to five babies in ten can contract their mother's disease through the birth process. So during his second year in office, as the nation was beginning to right itself after 9/11, President Bush launched the $500 million International Mother and Child HIV Prevention Initiative[97] to prevent mother-to-child transmission of HIV/AIDS in the hardest hit regions of Africa and the Caribbean. This trilateral action was the world's first full-scale assault on the deadly disease outside the borders of rich nations. However, it was simply a warm-up for what the president would announce six months later.

As he introduced the prevention initiative, Bush said that HIV/AIDS "staggers the imagination and shocks the conscience." After the speech, realizing that he just took historic but insufficient action, he ordered White House deputy chief of staff Josh Bolten to give Fauci his next assignment: to think big. Bolten then sent the

[97] http://georgewbush-whitehouse.archives.gov/news/releases/2002/06/20020619-1.html.

health chief back to his office to design a strategy that would alter the course of the epidemic.

In the July 2012 edition of *Health Affairs*, health reporter John Donnelly wrote a gripping account of the planning process that led up to the grand strategy announced by President Bush in the 2003 State of the Union Address. With his marching orders in place, Fauci conferred with his talented deputy Mark Dybul who had been his collaborator in modest clinical trials in some African nations in search of a viable anti-AIDS prescription.

Against the headwind of conventional wisdom that any African remedy would be doomed to failure because of the high cost, insufficient health infrastructure, and cultural predilections, Dybul made repeated visits to the African sites to see what the data revealed. Remarkably, he found evidence in Uganda that African lives could indeed be saved. The work of Peter Mugyenyi of the Joint Clinical Research Center in Kampala mirrored the success enjoyed by Indiana University doctors working just to the east in Kenya. They were among the pioneering doctors treating AIDS in Africa and proving that healing was possible.

Fauci and Dybul costed-out various options dubbed Chevrolet, Oldsmobile, and Mercedes; the president and his staff selected the Mercedes option, aimed at treating two million people over five years. The plan also included preventing seven million new infections and caring for ten million patients per year. These goals were unprecedented, yet fully compliant with the president's mandate to "think big" and identify results to target and progress to measure. This thinking represented the fullest expression of Bush's compassionate conservatism: It was compassionate to care for the African AIDS patient, and conservative to demand results from the caregiver.

Bolten and senior White House aides tested Fauci and Dybul's plan with noted global health experts such as Paul Farmer and Mugyenyi himself. Mugyenyi made a lasting impression when he said the carnage of AIDS represented a moral imperative and it would be a catastrophe to allow so many people to die when they could be saved. Bush advisor Jeff Lefkowitz said that the president met with some Jewish leaders about the same time. One of them mentioned that FDR refused an appointment with his father, who was part of a delegation seeking protection against Hitler. He said that with Bush's moral clarity, millions of Jews would have lived. Lefkowitz reports that the president met with staff thirty minutes after that encounter and said, "We are too wealthy a nation, and too compassionate a nation, not to take this step. It's a chance to save millions of lives. We have to do this."[98]

In the run up to the State of the Union announcement, Mugyenyi was spending his days inside the White House reviewing policy briefs and speech drafts. When the president said that he was proposing "a work of mercy beyond all current international health efforts to help the people of Africa" and pledged $15 billion to the effort, Mugyenyi literally leaped from his seat in the House gallery. Reading the words scrolling across his laptop in Haiti, Farmer thought to himself, *The world has changed.*[99]

Years later, I listened to Dr. Fauci deliver remarks at the State Department, regaling us with a history of this plan (eventually known as the President's Emergency Plan for AIDS Relief, or PEPFAR). One tidbit that surprised me was a PowerPoint slide

---

[98] http://www.commentarymagazine.com/article/aids-and-the-president-an-inside-account.
[99] *Volunteering in America: 2007 State Trends and Rankings.* Corporation for National and Community Service, 2007.

depicting a much younger George W. Bush sitting in an earlier Fauci briefing, this one for President George H.W. Bush, on the emerging domestic health threat known as HIV/AIDS. Apparently the seeds for PEPFAR were planted more than a decade before they sprung to life in African soil.

An Unlikely Alliance

Before PEPFAR could take effect, it needed congressional approval following the president's State of the Union announcement. Standing in the way was the imposing figure of Jesse Helms, an unreconstructed Southern conservative who was fond of saying that foreign aid amounted to pouring money down a rat hole. As chairman of the powerful Senate Foreign Relations committee, he could do more than talk. He could stop the Bush plan before it even began.

Senator Helms was far more multi-dimensional than his public caricature, however. His opposition to foreign aid was not reflexive but rather a principled rebuttal of the Cold War strategy of deploying humanitarian assistance to win friends among corrupt regimes. His close friend, the evangelist Franklin Graham, eulogized him in 2008 by recalling Helms' confession at Graham's Christian Summit on HIV/AIDS that he should have done more for the suffering.[100]

The summit itself was a breakthrough in AIDS politics. Hosted by the conservative Graham and his Samaritans Purse charity, he made a confession in his own right. The son of Christian statesman Billy Graham said that evangelical Christians had not done enough to help people with HIV/AIDS. The *Baptist Standard* reported that Franklin Graham's 2002 "Prescriptions for Hope" summit in

---

[100] "Interview with Franklin Graham," *Frontline: The Age of AIDS*. URL: http://www.pbs.org/wgbh/pages/frontline/aids/interviews/graham.html.

Washington was "part Christian theology lesson, part AIDS education program and part pep rally for social ministry."[101]

It is one thing for Helms to be persuaded by Franklin Graham, a fellow North Carolinian and ally, but it was even more remarkable for the eighty-year-old, five-term senator to be lobbied while propped up on his four-prong cane backstage at a U2 concert in 2001. And it was actually U2 front man Bono who helped convert Helms to the Africa mission. Bono challenged the senator with Bible verses about poverty, notably Matthew chapter 25 ("I was naked and you clothed me"). The Senator was moved, and the stage was set for his partnership with Graham and his eventual legislative work on Capitol Hill.[102]

The congressional debate witnessed an uncommonly strong bipartisan set of leaders that championed PEPFAR's passage. Joining Helms on the Senate Republican side was Bill Frist, a U.S. senator from Tennessee and world-renowned heart surgeon who had logged many medical mission miles in Africa and beyond. Among Senate Democrats, John Kerry introduced the legislation with Frist. U.S. Senators Mike Enzi (R-WY) and Benjamin Cardin (D-MD) have both been instrumental in observing implementation and making improvements during reauthorization.

Thus it was a troika of executive branch, congressional, and cultural leaders (on the stage and in the pews) who moved the African AIDS epidemic front and center while the rest of the world either tearfully mourned or willfully ignored its victims. President Bush, Senator Helms, Bono, and Franklin Graham were among the American leaders who considered it an unacceptable crisis. Each believed that there was a biblical mandate to do something about it.

---

[101] http://assets.baptiststandard.com/archived/2002/3_4/pages/aids.html.

[102] http://www.guardian.co.uk/world/2002/mar/18/usa.debtrelief.

Faith was at the heart of the policymakers' motivation, just as faith-based groups were at the center of the program's implementation. A 2008 Gallup Poll taken in nineteen African nations indicate that 76 percent of Africans reported trust in faith-based groups, higher than any other organization including government and the police. For their part, the Bush administration knew that it needed to rely on indigenous charities to deliver the services, rather than depend on Western ones that would leave the villages when the program ended. Therefore, more than eight in ten PEPFAR grantees were African faith-based and community organizations.

Putting Ideas into Action

If the PEPFAR legislation was the largest health program ever aimed at the developing world, the task of building it on the ground presented one of the most demanding public administration tests in the modern era. To administer this break-the-mold global health program, Bush knew that it would require a leader who could manage complexity and achieve results. So, rather than predictably selecting a public health professional, the president looked to the private sector and tapped former Eli Lilly CEO Randall Tobias from Indiana. Named to his post at the rank of ambassador, Tobias was installed in George Marshall's old office at the State Department, where he eventually became the first-ever United States director of Foreign Assistance, with dual responsibility as administrator of the U.S. Agency for International Development (USAID).

Serving first under Colin Powell and later under Condoleezza Rice, Tobias was charged with implementing the Bush administration's vision of transformational diplomacy. This model was rooted in partnerships rather than paternalism, along with a blurring of the lines between the three "Ds" of foreign policy: defense, diplomacy, and development. The post–Cold War era makes it impossible to draw neat, clear lines between security interests, development efforts, and democratic ideals. American diplomacy in the twenty-first century is required to advance them in unified fashion.

The PEPFAR administrators soon learned that the connection between AIDS and hunger is deadly. Dr. Peter Piot of the United Nations, one of the world's leading authorities on AIDS, told American policymakers that when he was in Malawi, he met with a group of women living with HIV. When he asked them what their highest priority was, their answer was clear and unanimous: food.

Women account for eight in ten African farmers, and AIDS sufferers are often too weak to maintain even their subsistence fields, thus perpetuating the food insecurity cycle. Hunger also makes these women vulnerable to opportunistic diseases such as TB and the exploitation of sexual predators. This vicious cycle perpetuates some of the world's greatest health crises.[103]

The relationship between medicine and food is essential yet perilous. Many parents face the dilemma of deciding whether to feed their children today or pay for medicine to make themselves well for tomorrow. However, health can only be gained when food and medicine are consumed together. Jim Morris, director of the United Nations World Food Program, often invoked the Haitian saying, "Giving a TB medicine without food is like washing your hands and drying them with mud."

Morris and Tobias were classmates at Indiana University, and coincidently it was their alma mater's AIDS program in Eldoret, Kenya, that was one of the first to marry lifesaving drugs with food nutrition. Roger Thurow lauded this innovation in a *Wall Street*

---

[103] "The Challenge to Agricultural Extension Services," Food and Agriculture Organization of the United Nations. URL: http://www.fao.org/docrep/006/y4973e/y4973e06.htm.

Journal editorial titled "In Kenya, AIDS Therapy Includes Fresh Vegetables"[104] and credited IU-Kenya program director Joe Mamlin for teaching his patients how to farm. Two acres of the hospital grounds were made into a garden growing carrots, onions, cabbage, and fruit trees alongside a stream for drip irrigation. Says Mamlin, "In the United States, I can sit in my office and write a prescription. But here, amid hunger and such poverty, I can't just write a script. There are no calories in the drugs."[105]

During a 2007 faith-based conference my office hosted in Indianapolis, Morris called for a movement comparable to a new civil rights campaign, saying it is no longer acceptable in this fruitful planet for children to die hungry. There is an abundance of food available, but war and inadequate agricultural practices cause too many places to go without. This former business executive and establishment Republican, with self-deprecating humor, then spoke of how the job has turned him into a radical feminist.[106] As he traveled the developing world, he became in awe of the women who care for the children, work the fields and demand a better future.

Ending Malaria

The scope of the president's Emergency Plan for AIDS Relief was so massive that some of the other Bush administration global health initiatives were overshadowed. One effort provided treatment for 300 million people in Africa, Asia, and Latin America suffering from seven neglected tropical diseases. Another fight, this one against malaria, neared PEPFAR-level impact.

[104] http://online.wsj.com/article/SB117502793580250798.html.
[105] Ibid.
[106] White House Conference on Faith Based and Community Initiatives, Indianapolis, November 5, 2007.

"At least one million infants and children under five in sub-Saharan Africa die each year from the mosquito-borne disease."[107] This shocking reality was brought to our nation's consciousness when President and Mrs. Bush held the first national summit on malaria in 2006. Malaria afflicts 500 million people each year. In 2010 alone, it killed 655,000, the majority of whom were children under the age of five. Ninety-one percent of the deaths are in Africa. This infectious blood disease, caused by a parasite transmitted by Anopheles mosquitoes, was eradicated in the United States more than sixty years ago. Yet in Africa, every sixty seconds a child dies of the disease.

In June 2005, President Bush launched the President's Malaria Initiative (PMI), a five-year, $1.2 billion program to combat malaria in fifteen of the hardest-hit African nations. By the end of the Bush administration, PMI delivered lifesaving medicines and protective sprays and nets to over 30 million Africans. The international community and private sector (notably the Bill and Melinda Gates Foundation) joined the fight, resulting in 80 percent of the at-risk population placed under bed nets and more than one million lives saved in sub-Saharan Africa over the past decade. During this same period, three new countries have eliminated malaria, and another twenty-six are making rapid progress toward the same.[108]

The faith community has been an active partner to governments in working to end malaria. At a White House Compassion in Action roundtable, First Lady Laura Bush described the $30 million Malaria Communities Program,[109] which engages indigenous faith-based and

---

[107] The President's Malaria Initiative. URL: http://georgewbush-whitehouse.archives.gov/infocus/malaria/.

[108] Malaria Fact Sheet, World Health Organization (March 2013) URL: http://www.who.int/mediacentre/factsheets/fs094/en/.

[109] The President's Malaria Initiative. URL: http://georgewbush-whitehouse.archives.gov/infocus/malaria/

community partners as key allies to their national governments. Two examples noted by Mrs. Bush included the U.S. government's partnership with the 40 million-member Orthodox Church in Ethiopia and the Mennonite Economic Development Associates in Tanzania. Given their distribution capacity noted by Rick Warren, both institutions were recruited to cover wide swath of the populations with bed nets.

Another vital partner is the corporate community. Africa's rich oil fields have made oil exporters out of thirty-eight of the continent's fifty-four nations. It also means that the United States draws nearly as much oil from Africa (10.3 percent) as it does from Saudi Arabia (12.9 percent). ExxonMobil has been doing business in Africa and the Middle East for more than 100 years and is doing well by doing good there. Since 2000, ExxonMobil has contributed more than $110 million to eradicate malaria, reaching almost 66 million people with 13 million bed nets, training more than 100,000 health care workers, and funding three pediatric anti-malarial drugs.[110]

Admiral Timothy Ziemer is the U.S. Global Malaria Coordinator. It is his job to spearhead the federal effort while mobilizing faith-based and corporate partnerships in the same direction. Among the chattering classes, he is admired for surviving the transition from Bush to Obama. But in his long battle against malaria and needs in the developing world, he has survived much more difficult circumstances than Washington politics.

The Malaria Coordinator's Redemptive Fight
Head of one of the world's greatest humanitarian success stories, Ziemer is a survivor of the very disease he fights every day. As a child of missionaries, Ziemer's whole family contracted the disease in

---

[110] http://www.exxonmobil.com/Corporate/community_malaria.aspx.

Vietnam. His parents started a school, a church, and a clinic there, which is remarkable in itself but not uncommon activity within Christian missions circles. Founding a leprosarium is another matter. This was the radical type of work that gave Christianity its reputation as counterculture revolutionaries.

Reporter Emily Belz tells a powerful account of Ziemer's journey to the White House malaria effort in *World* magazine. As a youth, he watched his father bring a Vietnamese man with leprosy into their mission and thus back into society. When Tim came back to the United States for a college education at Wheaton College, his father was shot by North Vietnamese soldiers while he was attempting to move the critically injured to a hospital. The warriors then threw hand grenades into the missionaries' bunkers, and Ziemer's mother was the only one to survive. Welcoming her back to the States at Andrews Air Force Base, Ziemer recalled that his mother had written some verses on a piece of paper and handed it to him, which he recited to Belz by memory:

> "When upon life's billows you are tempest tossed / When you are discouraged, thinking all is lost / Count your many blessings, name them one by one / And it will surprise you what the Lord has done."

He then recounted the blessings she named upon her return to the States: the privilege of being married to Ziemer's father, having three children, serving the Vietnamese people, having received good medical care, and knowing Jesus Christ.[111]

Ziemer joined the navy and became a pilot, flying over 500 sorties over Vietnam—though he is quick to point out that it

---

[111] http://www.worldmag.com/2010/02/survivor.

was more patriotism than vengeance ("That's the Lord's business"[112]). He then squared off against Soviet subs before becoming a rear admiral with command of the military's largest fleet in Norfolk, Virginia. After retiring from the military, Ziemer became executive director of World Relief, a faith-based development group at the tip of the spear in fighting AIDS. He was there when the president appointed him as the malaria coordinator.

Ziemer and I were going through the White House hiring process at the same time, and he became one my closest friends in the administration. We traveled to Rwanda together, where his program had slashed malaria rates by 64 percent. Ziemer keeps a sign on his desk that reads, "If only Noah had swatted those two mosquitoes." Since that didn't happen, the president has ordered the malaria initiative to cut mortality rates by 50 percent. I have no doubt this SEAWOLF veteran will get the job done.

In Zanzibar, child infection rates have gone from 20 percent to 1 percent, and there is now talk of no malaria deaths worldwide by 2015.[113] Through a combination of strategies—spraying, nets, drugs, awareness—and a multiplicity of partners, malaria's status has been downgraded from one of the world's great killers to a rare affliction.

Taken together, the President's Emergency Plan for African Relief (PEPFAR) and the President's Malaria Initiative has been called "health diplomacy," or the "diplomacy of deeds." African public opinion of America skyrocketed during the Bush years, and many leaders were sorrowful about President Bush leaving office, even though his successor was the son of a Kenyan. This was not a political gesture. It was the sincere reaction of a group of people who entered the new millennium with no hope of winning the

---

[112] Ibid.

[113] Peter Baker, "Zanzibar's Example in Fighting Malaria," *The Washington Post*, February 19, 2008.

AIDS battle that raged across the sub-Sahara. Ten years later, they are confident in their future.

Relief Is Not Development

For all this global health good and the goodwill it generated, relief is not development. Poverty will only be defeated by self-generating and sustainable economic solutions, which brings us to the second major Bush initiative in Africa.

Just as Ronald Reagan once said that the best social program was a job, a new generation of voices is making the case that well-functioning free markets are superior to foreign aid in the fight against global poverty. Evidence is mounting in support of this view. The World Bank reports that, thanks to strong economic growth in such places as India, Brazil, and China, those living in extreme poverty—that is, on less than $1.25 per day—declined from 52 percent in the first year of Ronald Reagan's administration to 22 percent in the last year of George W. Bush's administration.

James Shikwati, founder and director of the Inter Region Economic Network (based in his native Kenya), insists that government-sponsored aid to Africa is doing more harm than good. He claims that the African countries that collect most of the Western aid are in the worst shape. In stubborn opposition to the billions poured in, those nations have seen a rise in poverty and distress.

While good intentions largely fueled the donor aid, Shikwati bemoans the huge bureaucracies, corruption, and complacency that arose in response. Ugandan AIDS physician Peter Mugyenyi —who played such a key role in PEPFAR's formation—puts it in similarly blunt terms: "It is neither practical nor moral for Africans to expect the world to solve their problems. It's not practical since it places Africans at the whim of donors nations' changing politics and not moral because Africans have the capacity to fend for themselves or at least acquire the requisite skills. Sustainability must be the operative word in international development."[114]

President Bush did not see the debate as an either/or question. He proved his generosity by investing $15 billion in PEPFAR. But equally important to the amount was the method of spending. He conditioned aid on strict performance measures, zero tolerance for corruption, and authority resting with the African leaders themselves.

Bush wanted to replace good intentions and parallel systems with strategic focus, measurement, accountability, and self-sustaining systems. This, in turn, displaced an entitlement mentality and victimization with empowerment and human dignity. It required placing trust in the African leaders and their people. As evidenced by PEPFAR, Bush knew the best leaders would welcome the opportunity to build for themselves.

His solution to spur private sector investment was called the Millennium Challenge Corporation (MCC). It was introduced as "a new compact for global development," causing greater responsibility for both rich and poor nations. The MCC provided billions of dollars of investments in exchange for qualifying African leaders hitting sixteen performance indicators in three broad categories: to govern justly; to invest in their people; and to promote economic freedom.

This program's big idea is that generous MCC funds would incentivize policies that grew local economies. The target countries would bear responsibility for their own plans, which were assessed by MCC, which then monitored progress toward goals. It was venture capital with strict due diligence.

---

[114] Remarks by Ambassador Randall L. Tobias, "The Private Sector Driving Growth," African Growth and Opportunity Act Trade Ministers Forum, June 6, 2006.

For years, the foreign-aid lobby has snickered at the United States' low percentage of Official Development Assistance (ODA) in light of our nation's overall budget. The U.S. government contributed $30 billion in aid to the developing world in 2010. While this amount was more than double the second most generous nation, critics harped that we were among the five lowest contributors as a percentage of budget.

In the annual *Index of Global Philanthropy and Remittances,* Hudson Institute's Carol Adelman offered path-breaking research that revealed a deeper story beyond government-to-government aid.[115] Beyond the $30 billion Americans contribute to foreign aid through their taxes, they give another $39 billion through private philanthropy. Also, foreign nationals earning American wages send back $95 billion in the form of remittances to support family members in poor countries. Taken together, these two forms of private philanthropy total $139 billion annually, which is more than four times the amount of government aid.

There are twenty-three prosperous nations that form the donor community in support of low-income economies around the world. *Index of Global Philanthropy and Remittances* reports that the twenty-three donor nations contributed a combined total of $575 billion in private support in addition to the $128 billion they supply in Official Development Assistance.[116] The point? *While the ODA matters, private dollars matter a whole lot more.*

For too long, Africa has been viewed as the Dark Continent, with outsized and seemingly intractable problems such as famine, AIDS, genocide, and hunger. This means that Africans are invited to international gatherings to discuss aid not trade. What the continent needs is

---

[115] http://www.hudson.org/files/documents/bjwa_15%202_adelman.pdf.
[116] Ibid.

a success story to prove that business can work there in order to change the narrative from despair to confidence, similar to the way the Asian tigers achieved new respect over the past quarter century for their economic growth. With a game plan modeled specifically on Singapore's success, Rwanda may indeed prove to be Africa's first economic lion.

Faith in Rwanda

CNN journalist and longtime foreign policy analyst Fareed Zakaria considers Rwanda to be Africa's biggest success story. In a column for *Newsweek*,[117] Zakaria recalls that one-tenth of the population was eliminated during the 1994 genocide, and Rwanda shared a profile with Somalia as "as poster child for Africa's failed states." Yet, now Rwanda is a poster child for success, thanks to average incomes that have tripled, implementation of a health care system that the Gates Foundation calls a "model," and a business friendliness that prompted *Fortune* magazine to run an article with the title "Why CEOs Love Rwanda."[118]

In *Rwanda Inc.*,[119] authors Andrea Redmond and Patricia Crisafulli describe how Rwanda's President Paul Kagame runs his nation as if it were a business. To Kagame, it is. His wise stewardship over foreign aid and his self-reliant, entrepreneurial approach to nation building has won the support of key Western allies. One such partner is former British prime minister Tony Blair, who set up a Kigali office of his Africa Governance Initiative to help execute President Kagame's strategies.

As noted in Chapter 2, Rick Warren deems ethical leadership to be among the most important ingredients for aspiring nations.

---

[117] http://edition.cnn.com/2009/WORLD/africa/07/17/zakaria.rwanda.

[118] http://money.cnn.com/2007/03/28/news/companies/pluggedin_Gunther_Rwanda.fortune.

[119] Patricia Crisafulli and Andrea Redmond, *Rwanda Inc.: How a Devastated Nation Became an Economic Model for the Developing World* (Hampshire, U.K.: Palgrave Macmillan, 2012).

When he fielded a call from President Kagame, stating his desire for Rwanda to be a purpose-driven nation, Warren was intrigued to see what that would look like in practice. When he found a leader who desired to build institutions to outlast his (self-imposed) term-limited presidency rather than personal enrichment, Warren unleashed his network of faith-motivated business leaders to rally around the cause of building Rwanda's economy.

My friend Bob Buford started sending me emails and articles during this time that tracked the progress of Rick Warren's network of faith-based entrepreneurs building businesses in Rwanda. He convinced me that this was one of the biggest global faith-based initiatives and that the White House should become involved in supporting it.

Rick Warren eagerly endorsed my proposal to host a White House faith-based conference in Rwanda's capital city of Kigali, and he secured President Kagame's participation. Meanwhile, our mutual friend Peb Jackson helped me recruit American business leaders. My team then sprung into action, working diligently with the West Wing and the State Department to arrange the funding and protocols necessary to host a large White House conference with a head of state in sub-Saharan Africa.

Held in March 2008 to complement the president's travel to Rwanda the previous month, our conference did not focus on what the United States government was doing for Africa. Rather, we celebrated the American private sector leaders who were turning their faith into social enterprise in Rwanda and the Rwandan public and private sector leaders who were forming strategic partnerships and executing many effective strategies on the ground.

President Kagame was personally involved in leveraging the American business assets. He formed a President's Advisory Council to fuel the business leaders' vision and direct their energy. Too often, foreign assistance is restricted to government-to-government officials talking to each other. When private companies or charities do become involved, it's often well-intended but misplaced because their efforts are not directed by indigenous leaders to the most needed or strategic investments. President Kagame's idea to meet with the top leaders twice a year—once in Kigali and once in New York during the annual United Nations General Assembly—was groundbreaking and offers a useful model for twenty-first century public–private partnerships.

The council is filled with leaders from various parts of the West with backgrounds in government, finance, development economics, health, nonprofits, and the church. The likes of Tony Blair and Rick Warren have rich global networks to tap, and both invest vast personal resources into their own strategic philanthropy. Blair's Africa Governance Initiative places top talent inside President Kagame's administration to grow the government's capacity to operate successfully. Warren's PEACE Plan is mobilizing hundreds of churches to deliver primary health care services.

Seeking a Triple Bottom Line

Joe Ritchie, Bishop John Rucyahana, Dale Dawson, and Scott Ford are four other council members that deliver some of the most impressive social entrepreneurship I have ever witnessed. Each man is motivated by his faith to pursue a triple-bottom-line business return: financial profit, Rwandan development, and spiritual growth. Their highly interactive working relationship in places like Kigali, Little Rock, and Chicago demonstrates that the global economy works as fast in third-world development as it does in strictly commercial ventures.

Joe Ritchie grew up on the mission field in Afghanistan and has continued a life of grand adventure ever since. He revolutionized the options market by pioneering a computer-driven trading technique, and he collaborated with his friend Steve Fossett in breaking four world air-speed records formerly held by famed aviator Chuck Yeager.

Kagame first called on Ritchie to co-chair his Presidential Advisory Committee, and next he had something a little more day-to-day in mind. He asked the Chicago billionaire with his far-reaching global business network to serve as the first CEO of the Rwandan Development Board (RDB).

Following Singapore's playbook, the RDB was formed to advance microeconomic reforms and create a culture attracting foreign investment that would achieve 15 percent plus growth annually. As reward for the RDB's early action, the World Bank moved Rwanda up seventy-six places on its list of best places to do business in the developing world. This was the greatest year-to-year improvement that any country had ever accomplished. Rwanda is now ranked the second best place to do business among all low-income nations, and it is ranked ahead of the BRIC nations: Brazil, Russia, India, and China.[120]

Ritchie was soon joined in Kigali by a Little Rock entrepreneur named Dale Dawson. Bob Buford helped Dawson make sense of his inner emptiness while he was at the pinnacle of his investment banking career. As author of the bestselling book *Halftime*,[121] Buford himself was mentored by Peter Drucker in the transition from the marketplace to the social sector. Now Buford is leading others on their journey from success to significance, and no one has done it better than Dawson.

---

[120] http://www.sagamoreinstitute.org/library-article/fast-tracking-rwandas-development-a-view-from-inside-paul-kagames-government/.

[121] Bob Buford, *Halftime: Changing Your Game Plan from Success to Significance* (Grand Rapids: Zondervan, 2011).

Bishop John Rucyahana picked up where Buford left off with Dawson. Bishop John is an ethnic Tutsi whose family suffered death and destruction in the 2004 Rwandan genocide. He rejected hatred and instead become the leading force for national reunification as president of the National Unity and Reconciliation Commission. In addition to his role as church leader and restorative justice advocate, he founded the Sonrise School, where orphans of the genocide and other needy but promising students achieve outsize academic success.

As Dawson sat across the table from Bishop John for the first time, he was overwhelmed with the notion that this man of God was also one of the best entrepreneurs he had ever met. The two soon realized that Rucyahana's school could not be the finish line. Sonrise students could go from illiteracy to qualifying for admission to the best schools in the West, but the local economy needed to grow for them to return to Rwanda.

Dawson formed a nonprofit called Bridge2Rwanda to help students like Sonrise's graduates attend college while simultaneously growing businesses across Rwanda. Their first venture was the creation of Urwego Opportunity Bank in order to provide microenterprise capital and serve 95 percent of Rwandans who never set foot in a bank.

Employing a technique Dawson would later refer to as "borrowed talent," he recruited his friends and Little Rock finance experts Dabs Cavin and Todd Brogdon to move their families to Kigali to build the bank operations. It is now a $15 million annual enterprise—and so well-managed that Visa selected Urwego as its portal to begin their African lending practice.[122]

Scott Ford is another Little Rock businessman who President Kagame recruited to the President's Advisory Council because of

---

[122] Patricia Crissafulli and Andrea Redmond, *Rwanda, Inc.* (New York: Palgrave MacMillan, 2012).

his experience as CEO of telecommunications giant Alltel. With no vast natural resources and poor infrastructure, Kagame identified information and technology as the nation's leading economic development goal. Ford supplied needed wisdom and strategy on that front, but his entrepreneurial skills has also helped Rwanda exploit one of its few natural assets.

Rwandans are not coffee drinkers, but they grow some of the best coffee beans on the planet. At the Spring 2009 meeting of the council, President Kagame tasked a due diligence team to find the most important investment target. They selected coffee because of Rwanda's quality product and because it was the second largest dollar-traded commodity in the world. A case study analysis by the ISOKO Institute noted that other virtues included "a liquid market with a global demand, and there were only two well-capitalized players in the capital-intensive industry."[123] Scott Ford had found his playing field.

Ford founded Rwanda Trading Company to achieve the high market returns needed for the national economy but also to advance his social agenda. Since Rwanda has 500,000 coffee farms, the industry affected more lives than any other industry. This allowed Ford to build a business model that was attractive to foreign investors and African entrepreneurs at the same time, while demonstrating that good business invests in people rather than exploiting them. The company offers a vertically integrated supply chain that won more than 20 to 30 percent above average earnings and cross-training his employees to prove that investing in people is the right thing and the smart thing to do.[124]

[123] http://isoko-institute.org/world-changers/an-american-dream-for-africa.
[124] Mark Darrough, "An American Dream for Africa," How We Made it in Africa (2011) URL: http://www.howwemadeitinafrica.com/an-american-dream-for-africa/12347/.

Partnership, Not Paternalism

The stories of Ritchie, Rucyahana, Dawson, and Ford illuminate the path to Africa's renaissance. The policies of MCC and the culture change within Rwanda have created the best environment to do business in Africa, but these accomplishments are simply a means to an end. The true measure of success is education, capital investment, and jobs. Human capital is Africa's most important asset, and it has been underdeveloped for far too long.

In his remarks at our White House conference, President Kagame said that faith-based groups advance Rwanda's well-being by comprising more than 30 percent of Rwanda's health care facilities. In recognition of the American and African faith-based entrepreneurs who also shared their stories at the conference, Kagame signaled his preferred future when he said, "In Africa today ... trade and investment, not aid, are the pillars of development."[125]

President Kagame concluded his remarks to us with a robust vision for government, business, and faith-based groups to work as co-equal partners. "The more these constituencies act in unison," he said, "the more effective the results." Rick Warren affirmed the president's sentiment by stating, "This conference is about partnership, not paternalism."[126]

Following the event, Rick Warren invited me, along with Cynthia McFadden of ABC's *Nightline* and others, to tour his health care project in the Western Province community of Kibuye. Our helicopter landed in the stadium where 10,000 Tutsis had been murdered during the genocide. Merely fourteen years after that horrific episode, we were greeted by an excited and hopeful community, grateful for an American church's generosity and confident in their ability to chart their own future.

---

[125] White House Conference on Faith-Based and Community Initiatives, Rwanda, March 31, 2008.
[126] Ibid.

6

THE GREAT CHURCH
AND STATE DEBATE

The two religious liberty clauses of the U.S. Constitution's First Amendment adhere to a delicate balance. America's founding fathers rejected the state-sponsored religion of Europe and thus added a plank that protected its citizens from government forcing them to adopt a certain religion. Yet, for citizens to be fully free, they needed to add another plank that protected them against religious oppression as well.

The faith-based initiative had a similarly delicate balance to maintain. Of course, we needed to perch safely on both First Amendment planks anytime government funding was involved. But the bigger question was how to celebrate the public good that was created by private acts of faith while also honoring those who serve others out of goodwill.

President Bush often said that all of us are equally American, whether of one faith, different faiths, or no faith at all. He would speak of how we are a *great nation* because we're a *good nation,* and that we serve our country collectively by serving our communities personally. At dozens of White House conferences around the country designed to strengthen nonprofits and volunteers for such service, the president delivered all of these messages with zeal.

Echoing his original "Duty of Hope" speech cited in this book's Introduction, the president honored those who chose to be active citizens rather than passive spectators in our communities. While the message was not tailored for a faith-based audience, neither did it shy away from the unique contribution or outsized impact in giving and serving by the faith community.

The sight of Mr. Bush standing at the podium bearing the presidential seal and thanking the faithful for their service made faith-based groups feel welcomed in the public square. It also prompted a lawsuit from the Freedom From Religion Foundation who thought the president had no business engaging the faith factor in solving America's social problems.

It was not a new debate.

What Adams and Jefferson Wrought

The contest over right-sizing the shape of religion in American society goes all the way back to the Mayflower Pilgrims. They had fled England in search of a land where they could practice their faith in freedom. The reign of King James I (1603–1625) united the English and Scottish crowns but divided the faithful. He harshly persecuted Catholics as well as Protestant Puritans and Separatists. Archbishop of Canterbury William Laud added fuel to the fire of anti-Puritan sentiment, which subsequently accelerated the Puritans' exodus to America. So the story of church and state in the New World begins with the landing of the pilgrims in 1620.

Over the next 150 years, the early settlers, and eventually the revolutionaries, held differing religious beliefs. They generally agreed, though, that religion was necessary to promote civic virtue, social order, and the trustworthy markets necessary to the new republic. In short, if citizens were to govern themselves, they needed moral people, and morality was bolstered by religion.

Two hundred years after they arrived, a French visitor to America named Alexis de Tocqueville described religion as "the first of America's political institutions." Tocqueville recognized that America, for better or worse, was infused with faith. "I do not know whether all Americans have a sincere faith in religion— for who can search the human heart?—but I am certain that they hold it to be indispensable to the maintenance of republican institutions."[127]

Take John Adams, for example. A faithful Congregationalist who had notable influence in establishing America's national creed, he believed that the world owed most to the Hebrews for the idea that all people and nations are under divine judgment. In fact, he argued that this is what makes civilizations possible, thus necessitating the checks and balances required for self-government.

In what surely constitutes one of the most talented committees of all time, the Continental Congress of 1776 appointed Benjamin Franklin, Thomas Jefferson, and John Adams to design a Great Seal for the new nation. The committee members' initial recommendations reveal a high regard for religion and the influence of the Bible on their worldview.

Franklin proposed the motto, "Rebellion to Tyrants Is Obedience to God," and instructed the artist to depict an image of Moses overwhelming Pharaoh with sun rays resting on Moses to show him in God's favor. Jefferson similarly drew on a biblical allegory by suggesting a scene depicting the children of Israel traversing the wilderness, led by a cloud by day and pillar of fire by night.

It was the best-known Christian of the group, John Adams, who chose the secular alternative. Adams was inspired by the painting known as *Judgment of Hercules*, in which the Greek

---

[127] Alexis De Tocqueville, *Democracy in America* (Oxford University Press, 1947) p. 334.

mythical hero is forced to choose among two paths: the flowery path of self-indulgence or the rugged path to selflessness, duty, and honor.[128]

Fast-forward to the election of 1800. During George Washington's two terms as president, Adams served as vice president and Jefferson as secretary of state, but they had fundamental differences about government. After Washington refused to run for a third term, Adams and Jefferson squared off against one another. Adams was supported by Alexander Hamilton's Federalist Party, and Jefferson by the Democratic-Republicans. Adams' slim victory (71 to 68 electoral votes) set the stage for a rematch four years later in which Jefferson prevailed.

Their arguments focused on the role of government. Adams favored a strong, centralized state, and Jefferson defended states' rights. Among the issues that flowed from this debate is whether government had anything to say to religion. So it was that the campaign of 1800 was the first to make religion a political wedge issue.

Misunderstanding Jefferson

During the Revolutionary War, a National Day of Prayer had been adopted by the Continental Congress and authorized by President Washington to acknowledge the "Hand of Providence" in our aspiring nation's struggle for independence. President Adams decreed a similar national prayer observance during the 1798 undeclared war with France.

Jefferson opposed these federally sanctioned prayer days. Many believed then, and even still today, that Jefferson wanted to destroy religion all together. Some New England women even buried their

---

[128] http://www.greatseal.com/committees/firstcomm/.

Bibles when Jefferson won the election, fearing they might be prosecuted for their faith.

But Jefferson wasn't against prayer and religion; he was against religion seemingly imposed on the people by the federal government. Although he opposed national days of prayer, he was a staunch believer both in prayer and states' rights—so much so that he sponsored legislation in Virginia requiring "every minister of the gospel" to hold church services for public fasting and thanksgiving. Jefferson went on to draft the Virginia Statute for Religious Freedom, legislation he considered to be the second-most important he had ever created. Jefferson himself was so proud of this document that he instructed his epitaph to include it rather than his presidency: "Author of the Declaration of Independence and the Statute of Virginia for Religious Freedom, third president of the United States, and founder of the University of Virginia."

Though Jefferson was a skeptic when it came to core Christian precepts such as Jesus' divinity, he won points with Evangelical Baptists, who were marginalized in the northern colonies. In the Connecticut Valley, for instance, the Congregational Church was the official state religion, causing discrimination against Baptists and other minority religions. The Danbury Baptist Association, which was a consortium of two dozen churches from that region, was tired of having its members' taxes go toward paying the Congregationalist pastors' salaries. They wrote a congratulatory letter to Jefferson, the newly elected president, thanking him for his stand against religious oppression.[129]

Jefferson was likewise grateful for the Baptists' support. In our modern age, when American presidents receive more than 50,000 letters every week, it's hard to imagine that our early presidents

---

[129] Refer to Appendix D for a list of state-sponsored churches in early American history.

responded to letters received over the transom. It took Jefferson three months to thank the Danbury Baptists for their support, but his response would give shape to American jurisprudence for decades to come:

> To messers. Nehemiah Dodge, Ephraim Robbins, & Stephen S. Nelson, a committee of the Danbury Baptist association in the state of Connecticut.
>
> Gentlemen
> The affectionate sentiments of esteem and approbation which you are so good as to express towards me, on behalf of the Danbury Baptist association, give me the highest satisfaction. My duties dictate a faithful and zealous pursuit of the interests of my constituents, & in proportion as they are persuaded of my fidelity to those duties, the discharge of them becomes more and more pleasing.
>
> Believing with you that religion is a matter which lies solely between Man & his God, that he owes account to none other for his faith or his worship, that the legitimate powers of government reach actions only, & not opinions, I contemplate with sovereign reverence that act of the whole American people which declared that their legislature should "make no law respecting an establishment of religion, or prohibiting the free exercise thereof," thus building *a wall of separation between Church & State*. Adhering to this expression of the supreme will of the nation in behalf of the rights of conscience, I shall see with sincere satisfaction the progress of those sentiments which tend to restore

to man all his natural rights, convinced he has no natural right in opposition to his social duties.

I reciprocate your kind prayers for the protection & blessing of the common father and creator of man, and tender you for yourselves & your religious association, assurances of my high respect & esteem.

Th Jefferson Jan. 1. 1802.[130]

After affirming the First Amendment's protections against a state-sponsored church (Establishment Clause) and advocating for religious liberty (Free Exercise Clause), Jefferson inserted his reference to the "wall of separation between church and state." American University law professor Daniel Dreisbach notes that although the terms "separation" and "non-establishment" are conflated today, they had distinct meaning in 1802.[131]

Indeed, the Danbury Baptists themselves would have been comforted by the non-establishment of a state religion, yet they would have resisted any effort to wall off religious influence in society. Since he was writing an agreeable letter to his Danbury interlocutors, Jefferson would have been tuned into their resentment over a state-sponsored church. Hence his comfort in attaching the wall metaphor to reinforce their convictions against establishment of religion, since the only restriction in the First Amendment's language is actually toward the state.

The distinction between establishment and separation may have been clear to Jefferson and the Danbury Baptists, but their

[130] Thomas Jefferson's letter to the Danbury Baptists, 1802.

[131] Daniel Dreisbach, *Thomas Jefferson and the Wall of Separation between Church and State* (New York: NYU Press, 2003).

correspondence would become the object of debate between lawyers for decades to come.

The Supreme Court Constructs the Wall of Separation in Jefferson's Name

The Jefferson–Danbury letters may have been lost to history were it not for a couple of Supreme Court cases—one involving Mormon polygamy in 1879 and another one concerning Catholic schools in 1947.

In Reynolds v. United States, the Supreme Court considered whether the First Amendment's Free Exercise Clause protected one of Brigham Young's protégé's from marrying a second wife. Young himself requested the union for the explicit reason of challenging the Morrill Anti-Bigamy Act adopted in 1862 in opposition to the Mormon religious practice of plural marriage.

It was in the Reynolds' deliberation that the Supreme Court jurists studied the history of religious freedom during the nation's first 100 years. This search revealed Jefferson's letter to the Danbury Baptists, and the Court's eventual ruling declared that the letter "may be accepted almost as an authoritative declaration of the scope and effect of the [first] amendment thus secured."[132]

Jefferson's metaphor returned to the Supreme Court over a half century later when a New Jersey taxpayer named Arch R. Everson filed suit against his local school district for providing bus service to Catholic schools. In Everson v. Board of Education (1947), the Court considered whether the parents of parochial school children—96 percent of the schools were Catholic—should benefit from the same services afforded parents of public school students.

---

[132] Daniel Dreisbach, *Thomas Jefferson and the Wall of Separation between Church and State* (New York: NYU Press, 2003).

In a 5–4 vote, the Supreme Court found the New Jersey reimbursement policy to be constitutional because it was designed to benefit all school children (foreshadowing the school vouchers movement another half century later) and not any particular religious function. Writing for the majority, Justice Hugo Black gave faith-based causes a Pyrrhic victory by resuscitating Jefferson's letter:

> "Neither a state nor the Federal Government can, openly or secretly, participate in the affairs of any religious organizations or groups and vice versa. In the words of Jefferson, the clause against establishment of religion by law was intended to erect 'a wall of separation between church and State.'"[133]

Religious liberty would go on trial in many cases in the decades to follow, and Black's injunction of Jefferson's wall metaphor would be a useful precedent for those seeking to discriminate against faith-based groups. Everson's challenge to Catholic education, while unsuccessful, fit an ongoing backlash against Catholics that began during the rise of Catholic immigration in the mid-to-late 1800s.

In 1875, Speaker of the U.S. House of Representatives James G. Blaine proposed a constitutional amendment barring the state funding of religious schools. His arrows were aimed directed at the Catholic schools rising amid the swell of Irish immigration. His effort failed to become an amendment to the U.S. Constitution, but it was eventually adopted by thirty-eight states and known collectively as the Blaine Amendments.

The Blaine language at the state level is uniform and harsh: each contains language including some form of restraint against state money being "be appropriated to, or used by, or in aid of any

---

[133] Board of Education v. Allen, 392 U.S. 236, 1968.

sectarian, church, or denominational school."[134] A recent Supreme Court case underscored how little wiggle room this provides modern jurists.

Joshua Davey enrolled in Northwest College under a state-supported Promise Scholarship offered by the Washington state legislature to all graduates of state high schools graduating in the top 15 percent of their class and scoring 1,200 on the SAT or 27 on the ACT. Davey clearly met this criteria.

Yet, when he declared a double major in business and pastoral ministries at Northwest, his Promise Scholarship was revoked. The school invited him to maintain the scholarship by dropping the ministry major. Davey refused and brought suit, which allowed the courts to consider its merits via both the Free Exercise and Establishment Clauses.

The U.S. Supreme Court sided with the state in Locke v. Davey (2004) due to the state's plainly written constitutional language stating that "no public money or property shall be appropriated for or applied to any religious worship, exercise or instruction." The Becket Fund for Religious Liberty notes, "The amici contend that Washington's Constitution was born of religious bigotry because it contains a so-called 'Blaine Amendment,' which has been linked with anti-Catholicism...(however) the Blaine Amendment's history is simply not before us."[135]

National journalists, ranging from the liberal E.J. Dionne of the *Washington Post* to conservative Marvin Olasky of *World* magazine, supported Davey in his petition. Other recent Supreme Court cases, such as Zelman v Simmons-Harris and Mitchell v Helms, continue to take aim at Blaine, but none have been able to erase the bigoted

---

[134] Delware Const. amend. X. Sec. 3.

[135] Locke v. Davey, 540 U.S. 712, 2004.

history and lasting legacy of sanctioned religious discrimination. To quote from the Mitchell decision, this "shameful pedigree" and "doctrine born of bigotry should be buried now."[136]

Rebirth of the Church and State Debate

While Jefferson's focus was on protecting individual Americans from federally imposed religion, John F. Kennedy added his own bricks to Mr. Jefferson's wall 150 years later in attempt to show how his faith did *not* affect his politics. In a speech drafted by his aide, Ted Sorenson, attempting to calm Blaine-style fears, Kennedy said, "The separation of church and state is absolute." He then beseeched voters to judge him on his fourteen years in Congress—notably his opposition for public funding of religious schools and, more pointedly, his refusal to support an ambassadorship to the Vatican. "I do not speak for the church, and the church does not speak for me."[137] There would be no line of official communication, let alone authority, between Washington and Rome during a Kennedy presidency.

First Jefferson, then Blaine, and later Kennedy—each for dramatically different, even opposite, political motives—bent American law and policy in the direction of less religion in the public square. The reversal of this trend was sparked by a peanut farmer from Georgia who claimed to be a "born again" Christian while running for president in the 1970s, fueled by a Religious Right movement in the 1980s, and eventually given language by a great essay and a provocative book.

The essay was called "The Naked Public Square." Written against the backdrop of the 1984 campaign, which was hotly

---

[136] Mitchell v. Helms, 530 U.S. 793, 2000.

[137] John F. Kennedy speech to the Greater Houston Ministerial Association, 1960.

divided over questions about abortion and school prayer, author Richard John Neuhaus disputed the prevailing wisdom that America had become a secular society. He both criticized Jerry Falwell's Moral Majority for their dreams of a Christian America and lauded their objections to liberal attempts to exclude religious values from the public arena.

Neuhaus' essay reminded readers that 90 percent of Americans claim the Judea-Christian tradition. His eloquence with such phrases as "politics being a function of culture" and "religion being at the heart of culture" pointed to the realities of American public life. Careful to protect religious diversity in America, Neuhaus called for a "sacred canopy" that would check both the state and the church. His challenge to the church asserts that religious certainties must translate into public discourse accessible to nonreligious citizens and accountable to reason.[138] James Madison, author of the First Amendment, would have been pleased.

In the summer of 1993, newly elected President Bill Clinton was seen carrying a copy of fellow Yale alum Stephen Carter's latest nonfiction work, *Culture of Disbelief: How American Law and Politics Trivialize Religious Devotion*,[139] during his summer vacation at Martha's Vineyard. Carter's book shows how America is the most religious nation in the West, and at the same time, a nation that most zealously guards society against religious influence on our institutions in the name of pluralism. In our attempts to keep religion from dominating the state or vice versa, we've constructed political and legal cultures that force religious believers to sequester their faith—in Carter's words, "separation of faith from self."

---

[138] http://www.commentarymagazine.com/article/the-naked-public-square-religion-and-democracy-in-america-by-richard-john-neuhaus/.

[139] Stephen L. Carter, *Culture of Disbelief: How American Law and Politics Trivialize Religious Devotion* (New York: Anchor Books, 1997).

During an interview aired on PBS, the Yale professor built his case further. Carter said that popular media "too often either ignores the deep religiosity of tens of millions of Americans or treats it as something to be mocked."[140] This is the type of "trivialization" that Carter effectively demolished by citing such data as the fact that nine in ten Americans self-identify as religious.

Sweden is among the least religious nations in the West; a 2009 Gallup poll found that only 17 percent answered yes to the question "Is religion an important part of your daily life?"[141] India is among the most religious nations in the East. Echoing Carter's thesis, renowned Boston University sociologist Peter Berger likes to comment, "We are nation of Indians being ruled by Swedes."[142]

The New York Times, the *PBS News Hour,* and *Newsweek* each reported on the *Culture of Disbelief* as if unaware that they were complicit in the author's indictment. The month following Clinton's respite on Martha's Vineyard, *Time's* White House correspondents were granted an Oval Office interview, and their report began with a note about Carter's book on the President's desk, with the inserted jacket flap signaling Clinton's close examination.

President Clinton proved his seriousness when addressing a group of interfaith leaders in the state dining room, echoing the book's analysis that elites in government and the academy were working too hard to cleanse American society of religion. Said Clinton, "The fact that we have freedom of religion doesn't mean we need to try to have freedom from religion. It doesn't mean that those of us who have faith shouldn't frankly admit that we are animated by the

---

[140] *Think Tank with Ben Wattenberg,* PBS, http://www.pbs.org/thinktank/transcript108.html.

[141] Gallup Poll (2009) URL: http://www.gallup.com/poll/142727/religiosity-highest-world-poorest-nations.aspx.

[142] http://www.firstthings.com/article/2008/11/002-the-swedish-syndrome-32.

faith, that we try to live by it, and that it does affect what we feel, what we think, and what we do."[143]

Clinton Gets Religion

Clinton translated these sentiments into three policy initiatives that rebalanced the First Amendment and reshaped the arc of government away from discrimination toward equal treatment of religion in society: Religious Freedom Restoration Act (1993); Religion in Public Schools Act (1995); and Charitable Choice Act (1996).

> "The fact that we have freedom of religion doesn't mean we need to try to have freedom from religion. It doesn't mean that those of us who have faith shouldn't frankly admit that we are animated by the faith, that we try to live by it, and that it does affect what we feel, what we think, and what we do."
> —Bill Clinton, in a speech at a White House interfaith breakfast in 1993

The Religious Freedom Restoration Act (RFRA) was something Clinton inherited following a controversial Supreme Court case and subsequent legislation preceding his election. The case involved the firing of two drug counselors employed by the State of Oregon for using peyote, a controlled substance that has been used for centuries in Native American rituals. In *Employment Division v. Smith (1990)*, the Court ruled in favor of the state, with Justice Antonin Scalia, a conservative justice, claiming that the First Amendment did not restrict fair, generally applied laws that incidentally compromised religious practice.

---

[143] Clinton, Bill. "Remarks at a White House interfaith breakfast. (speech by Pres Bill Clinton) (Transcript)." Weekly Compilation of Presidential Documents. 1993. *HighBeam Research*. 1 Aug. 2009, http://www.highbeam.com.

Congress responded with outrage, prompting the introduction of bipartisan legislation by Stephen Solarz (D-NY) and Paul Henry (R-MI) and introducing RFRA. Clinton pledged to sign it during the 1992 presidential campaign, which aided its passage. It was upside-down politics: Liberals were supporting religious freedom largely to protect minority individual rights, while conservatives' were reticent to protect religiously sponsored drug use. This odd combination of interests merged in the unlikely support of both the American Civil Liberties Union and the National Association of Evangelicals.

In making the case for RFRA, Clinton said that while it was appropriate for government to restrict certain religious behavior, they had to have an extraordinarily good reason to do so. He signed the bill in a Rose Garden Ceremony in November 1993 and directed the general counsel of each cabinet department to designate a staff lawyer to ensure effective implementation of the law.

A Virginia Legacy of Religious Liberty

During a 1995 speech at James Madison High School in Vienna, Virginia, Clinton recalled how prayer was as common as apple pie in his Little Rock, Arkansas, schools. He used this event to announce the release of new Education Department guidance proclaiming the leeway public schools enjoyed in accommodating religious content. *Religion in Public Schools: A Joint Statement of Current Law* was created by "a broad coalition of religious and legal groups—Christian and Jewish, conservative and liberal, Supreme Court advocates, and Supreme Court critics—[who] put themselves on the solution side of this debate."[144]

---

[144] William J. Clinton remarks at James Madison High School in Vienna, Virginia, July 12, 1995.

Since presidents do not typically give big speeches to release federal agency booklets, the question lingers about how much the event reflected Clinton's desire to tweak America's "culture of disbelief" or his effort to list rightward as the 1996 elections drew near. Nonetheless, the document was a powerful directive in opening the public school doors wider to faith-based activity.

> "There are those who say that values and morals and religions have no place in public education; I think that is wrong. First of all, the consequences of having no values are not neutral, the violence in our streets—not value neutral."
>
> —President Bill Clinton at
> James Madison High School, 1995[145]

The James Madison High School location and namesake provided deep symbolic meaning to the proceedings. If America's desire for religious liberty originated at Plymouth, it matured in Virginia. George Mason of Fairfax, who took George Washington's seat at the Virginia Convention when the latter became commander-in-chief of the continental army, was the chief architect of the convention's Declaration of Rights, including and especially Article XVI protecting religious liberty. Convened in Williamsburg in May 1776, the convention adopted Mason's principles as part of Virginia's first constitution.

One year later, Jefferson drafted the Virginia Statute for Religious Freedom, which disestablished the Church of England in Virginia and guaranteed religious freedom for all faith traditions. James Madison used Jefferson's Statutes as his inspiration for the First Amendment to the U.S. Constitution. In his earlier *Memorial*

---

[145] Ibid.

and Remonstrance, Madison anticipated America's First Amendment protections for religious liberty by proclaiming an "unalienable right" publicly to worship God in freedom—without government meddling. "Religion, or the duty which we owe to our Creator, and the manner of discharging it, can be directed only by reason and conviction, not by force or violence."[146]

In his Virginia high-school speech, Clinton recognized the more than 200 religious and civic leaders who signed the Williamsburg Charter in 1988. That charter, eloquently written by Os Guinness in tandem with representatives of America's primary faith traditions, was named in honor of the city's role as the cradle of religious liberty, and it was presented on the 200th anniversary of Virginia's call for the Bill of Rights. The charter masterfully sets a course for the way a free society can navigate both promises of the First Amendment's religion clauses.

Clinton recounted the diverse set of national leaders who signed the Williamsburg Charter. Amid some good-natured laughter while reciting the list, Clinton noted the unlikely combinations of "Presidents Ford and Carter; Chief Justice Rehnquist, and the late Chief Justice Burger; Senator Dole and former Governor Dukakis; Bill Bennett and Lane Kirkland, the president of the AFL-CIO; Norman Lear and Phyllis Schlafly....(and) Coretta Scott King and Reverend James Dobson."[147]

Charitable Choice

Politics loomed largest in the final—and more far-reaching— Clinton-era church-state reform known as Charitable Choice. Famously campaigning to "end welfare as we know it" in 1992,

---

[146] Ibid.
[147] Ibid.

Clinton's welfare reform agenda stalled behind the doomed health care legislation. This opened the door for congressional Republicans to advance their own welfare reform bill in 1995–96, coinciding with Clinton's reelection campaign.

The GOP plan was vehemently opposed by the president's top welfare advisors, Mary Jo Bane and Peter Edelman, both of whom resigned in protest when he decided to sign the bill. Lost in the clamor about requiring welfare recipients to work in exchange for benefits, an obscure provision known as Charitable Choice was inserted in the welfare legislation. Sponsored by United States Senator John Ashcroft (R-MO), Charitable Choice was the clearest-ever policy expression of the dynamic balance; in the spirit of Madison's "true remedy," it sought neither preference nor discrimination.

In a 1998 keynote address to the very first national conference on Charitable Choice sponsored by the Bradley Foundation, my colleague, Dr. Amy Sherman, explained that Charitable Choice reflected the welfare reformers' desire to more readily engage congregations and faith-based nonprofits in serving the poor. In order to break the chains of intergenerational poverty, government needed partners who were in the business of life change rather than simply exchanging cash benefits.

RFRA and Charitable Choice were legislative solutions that signaled a shift away from the Supreme Court's early twentieth-century precedents that prohibited government aid to religious organizations deemed to be "pervasively sectarian." Up to this point, groups with strong religious orientation were prohibited from participating in otherwise widely available public programs. This pervasively sectarian doctrine required the courts to examine the religious beliefs and practices of religious organizations on a case-by-case basis to determine whether a "substantial portion of its functions are subsumed in [its] religious mission...."[148]

The problem was that government rules often put up extra legal barriers to faith-based participation. Charitable Choice established new rules for collaboration that leveled the playing field. Faith-based groups could retain their religious character (free exercise) while not proselytizing on Uncle Sam's dime (no state-sponsored religion or establishment).

Thanks to Charitable Choice, faith-based groups are entitled to:

- retain authority over their mission, governing board, and prophetic voice
- have the right to maintain a religious atmosphere in their facilities
- retain the right to use religious criteria in employment decisions

Charitable Choice likewise protects the civil liberties of individuals receiving services from religious organizations by requiring faith-based providers to:

- offer services to all eligible participants regardless of religious affiliation (or lack of same)
- refer eligible participants to a secular provider if desired
- not use governmental funds for purposes of "sectarian worship, instruction, or proselytization," and make religious activities such as prayer and Bible studies clearly voluntary[149]

---

[148] 20 USC sec. 1066c.

[149] Excerpted from Amy L. Sherman, *The Charitable Choice Handbook for Ministry Leaders* (Washington, D.C.: Hudson Institute and the Center for Public Justice, 2001).

Bush's Level Playing Field

As governor of Texas in the mid-1990s, George Bush was a proponent of welfare reform and one of the nation's earliest adopters of Charitable Choice. However, it took the tragedy of burned churches and some institutional self-discovery to give him a robust anti-discrimination vision.

James Heurich had been tortured by drug addiction until getting clean thanks to a faith-based recovery program. Thirty years later, his pain came from the Texas Commission on Alcohol and Drug Abuse, which punished him for operating his San Antonio-based Teen Challenge recovery program facility with a lack of credentials; the commission's rules only extended licensing to treatment centers with professionally trained dependency counselors.

Teen Challenge operates under a different model. They prefer homegrown leaders such as Heurich who beat their addictions through faith in Christ. The Texas governor would have understood this type of supernatural life change, since he experienced something similar in his own life. However, he learned that it was his government's officials who were the antagonists in this story.

In response to Teen Challenge's demonstrated success rate, which hovered between 70 to 86 percent, the commission's John D. Cooke retorted, "Outcomes and outputs are not an issue for us.... If they want to call it treatment, then state law says they must be licensed." The governor quickly put a stop to that approach, and the licensing procedures were relaxed within six months as part of his newly minted faith-based commission that forged a better path for government-faith partnerships in the Lone Star state.

"We each bear a responsibility to do justice and love our neighbors, a responsibility that comes from God. We see no threat to promoting the general welfare when government contracts with faith-based social service organizations."

—Faith in Action: A New Vision for Church-State Cooperation[150]

From a policy standpoint, this discrimination remedy may be the official starting point for George W. Bush's faith-based initiative. But the wider vision for Bush's future White House enterprise was formed the following summer when then-governor Bush and Dallas pastor Tony Evans joined forces to support the victims of two church burnings in Greenville, Texas.

The inspirational Evans not only brought comfort to the residents, he also made a lasting impression on the young governor by making the case that church was essential to healthy communities. He explained that neighbors in need all across America know where to find faith-based healers when life gets tough. In the years to come, Bush would cite this repeatedly as the moment his faith-based initiative was given its shape and character.

Don Willett served as chief policy aide to Bush in the governor's office, and he authored the Texas report *Faith in Action: A New Vision for Church-State Cooperation*. As special assistant to the president, Willett drafted the very first two executive orders signed by President Bush. These orders created the White House Office of Faith-Based and Community Initiatives, similar faith-based centers at five cabinet agencies, and required the adoption of Charitable Choice provisions in those departments.

The executive orders also required the agencies to conduct a department-wide audit to identify all existing barriers to the participation of faith-based and other community organizations in the

---

[150] http://www.twc.state.tx.us/svcs/charchoice/faithful.pdf.

delivery of social services. The White House faith-based office, led by the Ivy League academic John DiIulio with expert support provided by Stanley Carlson-Thies, supervised the agencies' investigations and synthesized its findings in an August 2001 report entitled *Unlevel Playing Field: Barriers to Participation by Faith-Based and Community Organizations in Federal Social Service Programs.*[151]

The report revealed discrimination that had reached deep into federal government policies during the twentieth century. Consider the case of Boston's Old North Church, where two lanterns were hung to alert Paul Revere that the British were coming. The church, which currently houses an Episcopal congregation, sought $317,000 from the U.S. Department of the Interior to make the building more accessible. As a National Historic Landmark, it should have been an easy decision.

Not so fast, said Barry Lynn of Americans United for the Separation of Church and State. He warned that the "Constitution prohibits the turning the public treasury into a church building fund, and that's apparently what this (Bush) administration now wants to do." He couldn't resist going further saying that if Revere was still alive today, he'd "ride around the country, saying your tax dollars are being abused." Fortunately for visitors interested in Old North Church's role in history, the building got its repairs.[152]

Equipping Faith-Based Leaders

In total, President Bush ordered federal agencies to not favor or disfavor groups based on their religion, but rather award funds based on results consistent with the nation's bedrock principles of plurality, the constitution's foundation of neutrality and his administration's

---

[151] http://georgewbush-whitehouse.archives.gov/news/releases/2001/08/unlevelfield.html.
[152] *The Daily Gazette*, May 28, 2003.

insistence on performance. As detailed in the White House faith-based initiatives' final report, *Quiet Revolution*, the administration would eventually adopt a half-dozen executive orders, implement sixteen rules to ameliorate all the onerous barriers to faith-based groups, and improve grant-making based on clearly established legal principles. The administration would also design robust guidance materials to train more than 70,000 policymakers, applicants, and grantees for the first time ever on clear, constitutionally established equal treatment principles (see Appendices E and F).

The White House ensured a full-scale implementation of this guidance process through published documents such as *Guidance to Faith-Based and Community Organizations on Partnering with the Federal Government.*[153] This provided plain answers to common questions about the availability and requirements of federal social service grant programs. The booklet also provides dos and don'ts for faith-based groups receiving government funding. These reiterate the equal treatment principles in layman's terms, easily accessible to program managers. For example:

Q: If I cannot take government money to support religious activity, how do I separate our religious activities from our federally funded social service program?
A: A faith-based organization should take steps to ensure that its inherently religious activities, such as religious worship, instruction, or proselytization, are separate—in time or location—from the government-funded services that it offers. If, for example, your church receives federal money to help unemployed people improve their job skills, you may conduct this program in a room in the church hall and still have a Bible study taking place in another room

---

[153] http://www.ojp.usdoj.gov/fbnp/pdfs/GuidanceDocument.pdf.

in the same hall (but no federal money can be used to conduct the Bible study). Or a faith-based social service provider may conduct its programs in the same room that it uses to conduct religious activities, so long as its government-funded services and its religious activities are held at different times. If you have any questions or doubts, you should check with the official who administers your federal funds.

Q: Can people who receive federally funded services from us also participate in our religious activities?

A: Yes, provided that a few rules are followed. It may be that some people have chosen to receive services from your organization because it is faith-based, and they will be eager to participate. But faith-based organizations that receive direct federal aid may not require program participants to attend or take part in any religious activities. Although you may invite participants to join in your organization's religious services or events, you should be careful to reassure them that they can receive government-funded help even if they do not participate in these activities, and their decision will have no bearing on the services they receive. In short, any participation by recipients of taxpayer-funded services in such religious activities must be completely voluntary. For example, a church that receives direct government aid to provide shelter to homeless individuals may not require those individuals to attend a Bible study or participate in a prayer preceding a meal as part of the government-funded services they provide. But they may invite those individuals to join them, so long as they make clear that their participation is optional.

Q: What if religion is integrated throughout our program—can we still get government funds?

A: In most cases, no, because as a general rule inherently religious activities must be privately funded, separate, and voluntary. An exception to this rule is the use of vouchers which means the individual is selecting the service provider (free exercise) rather than the government.[154]

Jim Towey was appointed the second White House faith-based director in 2002 and was chiefly responsible for overseeing the implementation of the legal guidance and rules changes. His background as a lawyer, Florida state agency director, and Capitol Hill staff member proved invaluable as he led federal staff through the agency reviews and equal treatment policy compliance.

Towey lived the faith-based initiative before he directed it. A full-time volunteer at Mother Teresa's home for people with AIDS in Washington, D.C., Towey also served as Mother Teresa's legal counsel for twelve years. He often joked in speeches that the Blessed Mother liked to sue people, before rushing in with a "Just kidding. Just kidding." His work was largely relegated to dealing with people who tried to make money using Mother Teresa's image, such as the Nashville coffee shop that hawked t-shirts with her image and "immaculate confection" underneath. Towey told the *Financial Times* that he dreaded approaching her wheelchair to reveal her image on a cinnamon bun, but then he'd chuckle when recounting the story, mimicking her husky voice saying, "Sister Nirmala is now the chief. Put her face on the t-shirt."[155]

President Bush always got a laugh when rhetorically asking what kind of world we live in when Mother Teresa needs an attorney. He got the answer in part when his administration was sued over his faith-based initiative.

[154] Ibid.
[155] Caroline Daniel, *Financial Times*, Aug 26, 2005.

Hein v. Freedom from Religion Foundation

One of the main vehicles to distribute the "Dos and Don'ts" training to both government officials and nonprofit leaders was through dozens of conferences across the country. This is the action that raised the ire of the Freedom from Religion Foundation (FFRF), which saw a much more menacing objective in the conferences: the unconstitutional reach of government in support of religion.

Since we operated the conferences, the FFRF sued the White House faith-based director and the directors of the federal agency centers for using money appropriated by Congress in violation of the Establishment Clause. A district court in Madison, Wisconsin, ruled that the FFRF did not have standing to bring the suit forward, but an appeals court in Chicago reinstated their right to sue. The Justice Department petitioned the Supreme Court to hear the case, and certiorari was granted on December 1, 2006.

Oral arguments in the Hein vs. Freedom from Religion Foundation case were held in February 2007, and the ruling was heard four months later in June. This was a case argued on narrow legal terms that held far-ranging consequences. It was the first church-state case considered by the Roberts Court, and its 5–4 decision in favor of the Bush administration has become a precedent cited in dozens of court opinions. The Hein case is being taught in law schools for both First Amendment and separation of powers lessons.

Obama's Conflicting Signals

Then an Illinois state senator, Barack Obama burst on the national stage with a soaring speech to the 2004 Democratic National Convention, delivering lines such as "We worship an awesome

God in the blue states."[156] This rhetoric was a powerful new chapter following Jimmy Carter's reference to being born again and Bill Clinton's culture-of-disbelief corrective action. Welcoming religion in the public square was taking shape as a bipartisan and possibly even nonpartisan issue.

On the road to receiving his party's nomination for president in early July 2008, Obama issued echoed themes resonant with dozens of Clinton and Bush speeches on the same subject: "As I've said many times, I believe that change comes not from the top down but from the bottom up, and few are closer to the people than our churches, our synagogues, our temples, and our mosques. And that's why Washington needs to draw on them. The fact is, the challenges we face today... are simply too big for government to solve alone. We need an all-hands-on-deck approach."[157]

> "The challenges we face today... are simply too big for government to solve alone. We need an all-hands-on-deck approach."
> —Barack Obama, Zanesville, Ohio, July 2008

Upon taking office, Obama administration officials have sustained all the Bush faith-based grant-making policies based on constitutional law, but they have lessened the government's grip on ending religious discrimination.

In 2011, Department of Health and Human Services Secretary Kathleen Sebelius proposed a regulation under President Obama's new health care law requiring all private health care plans to cover

---

[156] Barack Obama, remarks at the Democratic National Convention, July 27, 2004.
[157] Barack Obama, remarks delivered in Zanesville, Ohio, July 1, 2008.

sterilizations and contraception. Calling it "an unprecedented attack on religious liberty," the U.S. Conference of Catholic Bishops (USCCB) issued an urgent call to action and pleaded their case to the White House directly.

In an article published by *First Things* in February 2009, former Bush official John DiIulio presciently foreshadowed the 2012 HHS contraception debate by exhorting the Obama White House that "Catholic Charities, Catholic hospitals all typically serve people without regard whatsoever to their respective beneficiaries' religions." The sentiments echoed Bishop Hickey from Washington, D.C., who said, "We serve the homeless not because they are Catholic, but because we are Catholic. If we don't care for the sick, educate the young, care for the homeless, then we cannot call ourselves the church of Jesus Christ." DiIulio concluded with the admonition that "if the West Wing phones start ringing off the hook with complaints from Catholic providers, Obama should pay special attention."[158]

The HHS mandate clearly represents a retrenchment in religious liberty, but it is more of an exception than a trend. In light of the preceding Clinton and Bush administrations' record, the Obama White House so far has left a light footprint on the historic arc of church–state law and policy overall. All signs point to a White House that continues to support faith-based action in the public square.

---

[158] http://www.firstthings.com/onthesquare/2009/02/obama-and-the-faith-based-init.

7

THIS IS OUR CITY

This book has celebrated President Bush's creation of the faith-based initiative to fuel a wider compassion agenda aimed at desperate human needs. As we've seen, the initiative brought hope, healing, and opportunity to millions of people, both here at home and abroad—particularly in Africa. Tens of thousands of prisoners who had paid their dues got invigorated support to make a successful transition back into mainstream society. Countless other vulnerable kids, abused women, struggling military veterans, and impoverished families were connected to resources and relationships that helped to turn their lives around.

Through smart government reforms as well as creative and bold new funding initiatives, faith-based and community nonprofits found expanding markets open to them, including federal grant competitions. In return, these organizations mobilized thousands of ordinary citizens to rebuild storm-devastated communities, turned juvenile delinquents onto new, life-giving paths, launched new businesses to create desperately needed jobs in distressed neighborhoods, built thousands of units of affordable housing, delivered health care services, rescued victims of human trafficking, and so much more.

This focus on problem-solving was what the faith-based initiative was about.

So, while it is a disappointment that the national media did not cover the White House faith-based story in its full form, the story is so much bigger than what we can see through the lens of Washington, D.C. The faith-based initiative never was and never could be only a "government" initiative. Ultimately, it is about citizens of faith—visionary leaders, social entrepreneurs, non-profit managers, private investors, and dedicated volunteers—who embrace personal activism for the common good out of a desire to share God's love for the hurting.

For the faith-based movement to thrive and grow, it needs to return its center of gravity—away from Washington to cities across America. The faith community is ready. As evidenced by *Christianity Today*'s innovative project, This Is Our City,[159] a new generation of Christians is modeling a distinctly evangelical civic engagement for the new century.

Taking aim at issues ranging from urban blight to innovative philanthropy, executive producer Andy Crouch explains that that there is something about cities that concentrates and intensifies the human experience. As author of the groundbreaking book *Culture Making*,[160] Crouch has become one of Christianity's leading voices on the need to create culture rather than condemning it or simply copying it.

Crouch thinks that cities are the best place to fulfill this mandate, and demographics bear him out. In 1800, only 3 percent of the world's population lived in cities. That number bumped up

---

[159] http://www.christianitytoday.com/thisisourcity/.
[160] Andy Crouch, *Culture Making: Recovering Our Creative Calling* (Westmont, IL: Intervarsity Press, 2008).

to 14 percent in 1900 and then swelled to 47 percent in 2000. Most developed nations have three in four of its citizens living in cities, with urban growth expected to continue its rise.[161] Crouch is calling on Christians to use their gifts and energies in all sectors of public life—commerce, government, technology, the arts, media, and education—to bring shalom to the city.

During the last year of President Bush's time in office, I was often asked whether the faith-based initiative would be continued following the 2008 national elections. I loved receiving that question because it enabled me to restate the questioners' premise. Clearly, as this book reveals, presidential leadership matters. But I always answered the question by saying that the faith-based initiative should return to its roots. It should be owned and operated by private citizens motivated by faith in countless acts of public service. And the primary reason is that people, not bureaucracies, solve problems.

Citizens have always been at the center of solving our nation's most complex human needs. As the French political philosopher Alexis de Toqueville observed, "When an American asks for the co-operation of his fellow-citizens it is seldom refused, and I have often seen it afforded spontaneously and with great good-will. If an accident happens on the highway, everybody hastens to help the sufferer; if some great and sudden calamity befalls a family, the purses of a thousand strangers are at once willingly opened, and small but numerous donations pour in to relieve their distress."[162]

---

[161] *Global Metropolis: The Role of Cities and Metropolitan Areas in the Global Economy*, Martin Prosperity Institute (March 2009)

[162] Alexis de Toqueville, *Democracy in America Volume 2* (Indianapolis: The Liberty Fund, 2012), 1005.

Reclaiming the American Dream

The faith-based initiative itself will continue to grow in the spontaneous order that Richard Cornuelle introduced in his epic 1965 book, *Reclaiming the American Dream*.[163] Against the two decade-long rising tide of FDR's New Deal, Cornuelle's book introduced the term "independent sector" and made the case that America's myriad volunteers could effectively solve society's big problems without management by the state. The sum total of America's private voluntary sector now stands at tens of millions of volunteers and hundreds of billions of dollars aimed toward our neighbors in need each year. Peter Drucker called such compassion America's greatest export, yet its scope and scale is often overlooked or taken for granted at home.

America's extravagant generosity—both in manpower and money—often finds its structure in the form of nonprofits. But why do we refer to nonprofits by what they are not? Sure, they don't deliver profits for privately held interests, but they do produce over a trillion dollars in revenue each year, totaling 5.5 percent of the nation's entire GDP.[164] More importantly, their money is spent on the public interest. In other words, they are "public profits."

The nonprofit sector is the fastest growing segment of American economy. With private giving hovering around the $300 billion annual amount, charity is big business across the states. Where does this amount come from? The vast majority of giving (73 percent) comes from individuals' annual gifts and another 8 percent comes from bequests. Foundations and corporations combine for only 19 percent.

Renowned management consultant Peter Drucker predicted the rise of America's nonprofits, partly as a natural outgrowth of his

---

[163] Richard C. Cornuelle, *Reclaiming the American Dream: The Role of Private Individuals and Voluntary Associations* (Edison, NJ: Transaction Publishers, 1993).
[164] Blackwood et al., *The Nonprofit Sector in Brief* (Washington, DC: Urban Institute, 2012).

self-described "knowledge-worker" phenomenon, but also because serving in nonprofits creates a sense of personal fulfillment. Drucker experienced this himself, and he used much of his later life researching and espousing the vitality of the social sector (as he called it).

Today's leading management consultants have picked up the baton. Jim Collins followed up his landmark business book *Good to Great* with a forty-two-page monograph called *Good to Great for the Social Sector*. Tom Tierney stepped down as CEO of Bain & Company in 2000 to build one of the world's premiere nonprofit consulting firms, Bridgespan. Bridgespan has more than 100 applicants for every entry-level job, which is the same ratio as Bain even though the pay is 30 percent lower. Drucker, Collins, and Tierney are helping give rise to what Tierney calls an "industrial revolution for nonprofits."[165]

If there is a face for this new career path, it's Wendy Kopp, the founder of Teach for America. Named as one of *Time*'s 100 Most Influential People in 2008 when she was forty years old, Kopp believes educational inequities among rich and poor are among society's greatest injustices. As a remedy, she proposed a national teaching corps idea in her senior thesis at Princeton. It failed to impress her academic advisor, who snorted that she was "quite evidently deranged."[166]

Unbowed, Kopp turned the idea into a nonprofit, drawing more than 15,000 of her generation's best and brightest who were willing to trade lofty salaries and the fast track for classrooms in distressed urban communities. In 2009, Teach for America received a record 35,000 applications for 1,400 openings, and it remains the largest recruiter on Ivy League campuses.

---

[165] Quoted in "New York conference spotlights a social sector enjoying tremendous growth and new opportunities," The Drucker Institute (2007) URL: http://www.druckerinstitute. com/link/new-york-conference-spotlights-a-social-sector-enjoying-tremendous-growth-and-new-opportunities/.

[166] Jeffery Kluger, "Wendy Kopp," *Time* (2008).

Not to be undone, the Boomer generation has discovered a renaissance in their pathway to citizen service. Unveiling such conceptions as encore careers and skilled volunteerism, workers in their prime are searching for the type of social significance popularized by Peter Drucker's protégé Bob Buford, who coined the term "success to significance." His bestselling book *Halftime* has propelled thousands of high capacity professionals to trade for-profit jobs for public profit service.

A Call to Service

So how does the president of the United States add value to this generational competition for social impact? Inspired by his father's Points of Light campaign and his own family's service ethic, George W. Bush's first step was a call to service. And the fitting occasion was our nation's darkest hour since Pearl Harbor: September 11, 2001. Unlike World War II, Americans would not be called to fight on the frontlines or ration goods on the home front. Instead, we were attacked for the values we represent, and therefore the president knew that we needed to reinforce our national identity by giving and serving in communities across America to preserve and extend those values.

Making good on his promise to Bill Clinton, Bush strengthened Americorps by making it a capacity-building engine for nonprofits. For example, Reverend Kevin Brown in New Orleans used Americorps volunteers to grow his Trinity Christian Church program tenfold and refocus his ministry on disaster recovery. This strategic investment resulted in 1,600 homes being rebuilt post-Katrina. At a ceremony honoring their success, Rev. Brown said, "Getting the grant to bring aboard these hard workers... was a blessing for my community. We are victims of this storm, but with faith in humanity and faith in God we are also victors."[167]

---

[167] Quoted in Laura Bush's remarks at the ServiceNation Summit, 2008.

After the most powerful earthquake in nearly half a century struck the Indian Ocean and hundreds of thousands lives were lost, President Bush enlisted his father and former president Clinton to raise $100 million in private donations. Following Katrina, perhas the most heartwarming donation came not from Wall Street, but rather a Ugandan refugee camp. Grateful for the kindness shown them by the American people, they wanted to do their part after hearing about the horrible flood damage. "We're the donors now," was their simple but inspiring message.

President Bush established the President's Council on Service and Civic Participation to help him pursue his 2002 call for all Americans to give two years or 4,000 lifetime hours to service.[168] Under the leadership of AOL co-founder Jean Case who served as chair, the main task of the council was awarding a presidential medal for every-day but exemplary volunteers. The council spurred its own innovation as well. For example, Vice Chair Michael W. Smith founded a faith-based youth program in Nashville called Rocketown that was one of Mrs. Bush's favorite Helping America's Youth success stories.

The council's big new idea came from Case, who challenged corporations to provide $1 billion in pro bono service across the nation. As nonprofits face increased difficulty in raising money while confronting ever-greater demand for their services, their leaders need to find cost-effective ways to do more with less. For their part, businesses must find better ways to recruit, train, and retain employees—who also expect their companies to be engaged in the community. The corporate pro bono movement meets both objectives with a single shot, and it offers much promise for improved lives.

The council hosted the inaugural Pro Bono Summit at the Harvard Club in New York City on February 8, 2008. Council

---

[168] George W. Bush. State of the Union (2002).

member Tony Dungy delivered keynote remarks and honored six companies who were exemplars in skills-based volunteering:

1. **Ad Council**—For over sixty years, the Ad Council has been the advertising industry's gift to our communities. Every year dozens of ad firms develop the pro bono creative that Ad Council places on $2 billion in donated ad inventory to get out critical PSAs.

2. **McKinsey & Company**—Since its inception, McKinsey has made pro bono a core part of their culture. Today, their 8,000 consultants provide 5 percent of their time to pro bono work. That is the equivalent of a 400-person full-time consulting firm dedicated to pro bono.

3. **General Electric**—GE has pioneered the in-house legal pro bono concept. Their leadership has enabled attorneys to realize that they don't need to be at a law firm to do it pro bono. Today, roughly 50 percent of GE attorneys participate in the program.

4. **Pentagram Design**—Pentagram, the gold standard of design firms, reports that 50 percent of their clients are nonprofits that they serve pro bono. Their pro bono work is widely recognized and is a significant part of what attracts their paid corporate work.

5. **Monitor**—Monitor, a 1,500-person consultant strategy firm, has partnered with New Profit, Inc., in Boston to channel tens of millions of dollars of pro bono consulting to well-vetted and high-potential social entrepreneurs. By working with New Profit, Monitor is able to focus their pro bono efforts on high-potential nonprofits at an inflection point in their growth. This maximizes the impact of their pro bono work.

6. **Harvard Business School Community Partners**—HBSCP works with HBS alumni on consulting projects for non-profits. In the Bay Area alone, they provide over $1 million per year in consulting to local nonprofits. They are making pro bono part of what it means to be an HBS alumnus.

7. **Time Warner**—Time Warner forged an innovative collaborative with the Taproot Foundation to use skills-based volunteering to provide much-needed assistance to local nonprofits, as well as a professional development tool for their employees.

More than 500 companies made $2 billion worth of skills-based volunteer pledges to the Billion + Change campaign, making it the largest commitment of pro bono in history.[169] Drawing from *Fortune* 500 companies to small proprietors, the leading pledge industries included financial services, communications/PR, technology, and architecture.

> "For progressive corporations, service is now an integral part of business strategy. It benefits nonprofit clients, enhances the attraction and retention of top talent, offers brand and relationship building opportunities and provides critical entrees into new markets—especially in developing economies."
>
> —Stanley S. Litow, IBM's vice president of Corporate Citizenship & Corporate Responsibility and president of the IBM Foundation[170]

---

[169] "A Billion + Change Inspires Largest Commitment of Pro Bono Service in History" URL: http://www.abillionpluschange.org/press_release/billion-change-inspires-largest-commitment-pro-bono-service-history.

[170] "A Billion + Change Inspires Largest Commitment of Pro Bono Service in History" URL: http://www.abillionpluschange.org/press_release/billion-change-inspires-largest-commitment-pro-bono-service-history.

Urban Entrepreneurs

A presidential call to service and innovative nonprofits go a long way to redeeming our cities, but the ultimate goal is to defeat poverty, not just manage it. Enter the new class of faith-based urban entrepreneurs who are erasing the bad part of town.

The economic distress of America's inner cities causes not only a crushing cycle of poverty but also crippling social problems such as drug abuse and crime. Harvard University professor Michael Porter suggests that a sustainable economic base can be created in the inner city. But it can only be done as it has been created elsewhere in society: through private, for-profit initiatives and investments based on economic self-interest and genuine competitive advantage.

In 2007, I traveled with the Commerce Department's Economic Development Administration officials to Houston's 5th Ward to award a grant to a faith-based group that was turning Porter's vision into reality. This neighborhood was settled by freed slaves after the Civil War and has long struggled with poverty and high crime patterns. It also produced Congresswoman Barbara Jordan, boxing champ George Foreman, and boasted a stylish clothing store called Caldwell's where a young man named Kirbyjon learned how to do business in his father's shop.

Kirbyjon Caldwell went on to earn a MBA at the prestigious Wharton School of Business at the University of Pennsylvania. Then it was on to Wall Street to work for First Boston before returning to Houston to join a regional investment-banking house. Three months into his new job, Caldwell says that he received a call to the ministry. Attempting to explain the nature of a religious call in his Wharton alumni newsletter, Caldwell says that he was "eclipsed by God's will. All I knew was I was supposed to stop selling bonds and start pastoring a church."[171]

---

[171] "Leading with Religion: Wharton Graduate and Megachurch Pastor Kirbyjon Caldwell Combines Faith and Finance," *Wharton Leadership Digest*, May 2007.

The banker-turned-pastor is an entrepreneur at his core. Much like Harvard's Porter, Caldwell deploys his business skill in pioneering investments to transform the economic infrastructure of his community. Caldwell likes to remind people that the original meaning of the word "entrepreneur" had nothing to do with money. It referred to the galvanizing of all forms of capital—intellectual, social, and financial—to pursue a common goal.

When pressed by others to defend mixing business and religion, Caldwell is forceful in response. "Faith and finance were never intended to get a divorce. Rather, God intended them to be in a healthy relationship. The Bible has more verses on money and commerce than it does on faith, prayer, heaven and hell combined.... God has blessed us to be a blessing to others, and that has an economic meaning too."[172]

It's fair to say that his Windsor Village United Methodist congregation has been a considerable blessing in the 5th Ward. The church's first big project was the 104,000-square-foot Power Center, a state-of-the-art complex that meets the needs of over 10,000 low-income families monthly. It includes the Imani School, J.P. Morgan Chase Bank, the business technology center of Houston Community College, the University of Texas-Hermann Hospital Clinic, more than two dozen business suites, government social services, and the fourth largest banquet facility in Houston. As we stood outside the multi-purpose church and service center, Caldwell greeted dozens of his parishioners by name. He may be busy doing deals with leaders across town, but it's clear that these are his people; their well-being both prompts his entrepreneurial zeal and serves as its measuring stick.

We left the Walmart-sized parking lot to tour the 234-acre multi-use community center that Windsor UMC is building

---

[172] Ibid.

next door to the church. Its main feature is Corinthian Point, the largest subdivision ever built by a nonprofit entity. It contains 464 lovely homes, 80 percent of which happen to be occupied by low- to moderate-income residents. Visitors would not be able to tell which among these nice homes qualify as "low-income" housing. The neighborhood also includes a YMCA, public school, Texas Children's Pediatrics Center, a community park, and an 8.5-acre commercial development. Finally, there is a half-million-square-foot community center, complete with a charter school, the NASA program (the space agency is in town, of course), a family life center, and a sanctuary. Caldwell calls it "a smorgasbord of spiritual and social services."[173]

Much like Caldwell, who transferred his investment skills from banking to community development in Houston, Herb Lusk parlayed his status as Philadelphia Eagles football star to a home-town hero rebuilding an impoverished North Philly neighborhood. During his playing days, Lusk was known as the praying tailback. Long before Tebowing became a national phenomenon, Lusk took a toss from Eagles quarterback Ron Jaworski and raced seventy yards for a fourth-quarter touchdown against the rival New York Giants. He took a knee in the end zone and said a quick prayer—becoming the first NFL player to do so.

Lusk made a commitment to himself that he would only play three years in the NFL and then enter full-time ministry. He began with few parishioners in a rundown part of town when he first stepped into the pulpit at the Greater Exodus Baptist Church. The congregation ballooned to 1,500, and the church has turned its blighted surrounding neighborhoods into an oasis amid North Philly's continued challenges.

---

[173] Ibid.

Early on, Lusk attempted to get a loan at the bank adjacent to the church. The bank said no; undeterred, Lusk was able to buy that bank a decade later. The People for People Credit Union became the second community development credit union in the state of Pennsylvania, much to the delight of then-Gov. Tom Ridge who pinned his hopes on the endeavor to spur urban revitalization. It also reversed the trend of banks vacating distressed urban neighborhoods like Lusk's.

People for People owns and occupies an eight-story building next to the church, which is filled with a charter school, a day care center, youth mentoring, a summer reading camp, and a banquet center overlooking the Ben Franklin Bridge—and the blight that shows how much work is still left to be done. The church's location on the corner of Broad and Fairmont is one of the worst in the city, but Lusk is fighting back with this nonprofit that employs 200 and operates with a budget of $10 million.

During the 4th of July holiday his first year in office, President Bush was invited to a block party hosted by Lusk in the nation's first capital. But rather than standing on the lawn at Independence Hall, the president ate barbeque outside Greater Exodus, played with kids from the 'hood, and socialized with the families of prisoners connected to the Amachi program. Bush returned to Greater Exodus three years later to deliver remarks on his new African AIDS initiative in recognition of Lusk's Stand for Africa campaign.

Caldwell and Lusk's stories reveal that people of faith often receive extraordinary vision for how to meld their spiritual beliefs with practical solutions to serve the common good.

Social Investment

Whether it's the entrepreneurs in Rwanda we examined in Chapter 5 or the stories of Caldwell or Lusk told on the previous pages, the lines are becoming increasingly blurred between business and social enterprise. This has prompted Carl Schramm, long considered one of the nation's leading thinkers on entrepreneurship, to say that *all* entrepreneurship is social. Acknowledging the widening popularity of the term "social entrepreneurship" since the mid-1990s, Schramm questions whether the modifier is needed. He's skittish about the term "social" because he fears it diminishes the regular entrepreneurs who "create thousands of jobs, improve the quality of goods and services available to consumers, and ultimately raise the standards of living."[174] As microfinance pioneer and Nobel Peace Prize winner Muhammad Yunus likes to say, "Income is the best medicine."[175]

Regardless of what it's called, the next generation is acting as if this way of operating is the new normal. The Praxis Nonprofit Accelerator program[176] targets Christians with high-growth, pre-scale nonprofits or businesses that are going after problems of considerable magnitude. After selecting a rotating class of fellows, Praxis offers world-class mentorship, a faith-based peer community, access to new capital, and creative equipping sessions at high-end private retreats in New York, Los Angeles, and Orlando.

Praxis is tapping into a growing market. The Kaufmann Foundation reports that 54 percent of the millennial generation want to start a business or join a start-up.[177] Praxis' leaders advance a gospel-minded entrepreneurship—in other words, a connection between faith and action in the marketplace that they refer to as "orthopraxis."

---

[174] Carl Schramm, "All Entrepreneurship is Social," *Stanford Social Innovation Review*, 2010.

[175] Quoted in "Subprime Lender," Emily Parker, *The Weekend Interview*, WSJ online, March 1, 2008; http://online.wsj.com/article/SB120432950873204335.html.

[176] http://www.praxislabs.org/nonprofit-accelerator/.

[177] http://www.kauffman.org/newsroom/millennials-want-to-start-companies-when-economy-rebounds-poll-says.aspx.

The organization is led by some of the leading-edge thinkers in evangelicalism today, including Josh Kwan, Gabe Lyons, and Dave Blanchard. Kwan comes from the emerging venture philanthropy field, as does another Praxis board member, Henry Kaestner, cofounder of Bandwidth.com. Kaestner has recently opened Sovereign's Capital, a $40 million fund created to invest in other entrepreneurs motivated by their faith. Kaestner is a leader within a movement called "business as mission," which is a faith-based version akin to the Billion + Change corporate pro bono strategies noted earlier. Therefore, his multiple bottom lines include helping Christian businesses extend their reach in the developing world as well as realize the social and financial impact of successful investments.

Another investor, Russ Hall, leverages the venture capital deal flows of Silicon Valley to help individual and foundations heighten their philanthropic impact. His business, Venture Works, has raised over $1 billion by incentivizing strategic philanthropy via tax breaks and marketing mission-centered investments to "do good while doing well." Hall notes that many of the Silicon Valley's wealthy population are nouveau riche and therefore lacking giving habits. His firm offers training and inspiration to make philanthropy more exciting and rewarding than second homes or other luxuries.[178]

Government is getting into the social investment act as well. British Prime Minister David Cameron is conducting an important experiment to support grassroots social projects with the United Kingdom's first social investment bank, Big Society Capital. Drawing 600 million pounds from bank accounts that have been dormant for fifty years and adding another 200 million pounds contributed by Britain's four largest banks (Barclays, Lloyds, HSBC,

---

[178] http://www.christianitytoday.com/ct/mobile/thisisourcity.html?id=104089.

and RBS), the fund will create a rational market for social innovation based on sound business plans. The best plans will be funded, and their success will draw investment from other sources for replication, just like any other market-based business.[179]

Cameron tabbed Sir Ronald Cohen to run the Big Society Bank. Cohen is considered the father of British venture capital and in 2000 he became chair of the Social Investment Task Force to investigate how to obtain higher financial and social returns from public investments. In 2007 he co-founded Social Finance to help establish the UK social investment market. Their signature product is a Social Impact Bond that the public sector can use to achieve upgraded services through outcomes-based contracts. Their first pilot aims at reducing recidivism among returning prisoners, since re-offending is very expensive to the government.

This is an experiment worth watching. No government funds were used to build the bank's assets; loans are delivered to nonprofits based on solid plans and according to strict measurements. The targets are all dire social needs that otherwise consume much tax-supported public expenditures. The social impact bond, or pay-for-success model, is taking root in the United States as well. Note: These are not financial bonds or debt instruments but rather contract-based partnerships.

The question of business and social good brings to mind the often-repeated phrase that government and nonprofits need to be run more like business. Rick Warren says that Peter Drucker once told him what that looks like in the context of the church. Drucker said that the function of management in the church is to make the church more churchlike not more businesslike. This

---

[179] Chris Gibson-Smith, Press Conference launching Big Society Capital at the London Stock Exchange (April 4, 2012) URL: https://www.gov.uk/government/speeches/transcript-press-conference-launching-big-society-capital-at-the-london-stock-exchange.

insight reveals that using business solutions to advance a social outcome is simply good business—regardless of whether your business is for-profit or public profit.

Great Cities Need Great Neighborhoods

A great nation needs great cities, and great cities need great neighborhoods. In the words of former St. Petersburg, Florida, Mayor Rick Baker, we need seamless cities where there is no longer a good part of town and a bad part of town.

As an ugly remnant of racial segregation, St. Pete has had a bad part of town since it became the terminus for a railroad that brought in droves of people looking to vacation or retire near the region's sunny beaches. Many African Americans arrived to help build the railroad, and others migrated there as the city developed, especially during its 1920s boom. Similar to other southern cities, the black population was confined to a discreet part of town where the black school, black hospital, and black housing were located.

Upon taking office in 2001, Baker gave this neighborhood an uplifting name—Midtown—and made turning around this blighted region a top priority. He partnered with Dr. Goliath Davis, or "Go" as he is called, an African American police officer who worked his way up to chief in the Midtown neighborhood that Mayor Baker was trying to restore.

Baker and Davis were relentless in their innovation. They sought to build a city park within a half-mile of every resident. They raised money from the private sector to guarantee free college to sixth graders who graduated from high school with at least a "C" average and who remained crime-free. Against the 50 percent dropout rates in urban areas, 93 percent of these children graduated from high school.

Crime plummeted, and city crews were ubiquitous in cleaning up the streets, installing streetlights, and paving sidewalks. Since Baker's 2001–2009 term in office, visitors are hard-pressed to locate the bad part of town. St. Petersburg is one city now.

Baker drew inspiration for his mayoral leadership from Steve Goldsmith, who achieved similar success in Baker's hometown of Indianapolis. Indianapolis added another chapter to America's urban revitalization story when the city played host to the 2012 Super Bowl. True to its civic spirit, it sought to show the world that it would be more than a game.

When cities host a Super Bowl, the NFL provides a $1 million gift to the community as a thank you. Called the Legacy Project, these funds typically go to build a youth center in an impoverished part of town. Indianapolis officials decided to build a youth center, too—but only as one part of a multidimensional, super-sized initiative to transform an at-risk neighborhood.

The Near Eastside of Indianapolis has been in a state of urban flux. The area contains Indianapolis' first suburb, where homes can still be sold for a half-million dollars. Yet, real estate prospectors can walk several blocks from the remnants of a gilded past to purchase a home on their credit card for less than $5,000. As the housing crisis swept through the nation in the mid-2000s, the Near Eastside led the nation in foreclosure rates. Its slide began twenty years earlier following two plant closings that resulted in thousands of lost jobs. Following the loss of discretionary income, three large shopping centers were shuttered, and the downward spiral ensued.

This mounting crisis fueled the imagination and "can do" spirit of the Near Eastside's residents, and they rallied together to build a quality-of-life plan. Indianapolis corporate partners teamed up with government and philanthropy to invest $150 million in the

Near Eastside Legacy plan. The majority of the money was spent rehabbing or rebuilding mixed income homes, but it also included expanded health care services and education programs, as well as the community's first fitness and wellness center. Funds were also directed to redevelop a two-mile stretch along the neighborhood's business corridor by upgrading facilities, recruiting businesses to fill abandoned buildings, adding bike lanes, and other strategies to fuel private investment long after the Super Bowl's klieg lights moved to another city.

Meanwhile, Indianapolis' downtown revitalization story is expanding. Visionary developer Gene Zink is leading a group of investors, including Warren Buffett, to raise $150 million to replicate an Atlanta model in the Avondale Meadows neighborhood just a few miles north of the Super Bowl Legacy project.

The Atlanta story began when developer Tom Cousins rescued Bobby Jones' home course, the East Lake Golf Club. The neighborhoods surrounding the once-famous golf course had deteriorated into one of the city's most crime-and-drug-infested sectors. Daily gun violence there led to the neighborhood becoming known as "Little Vietnam." City planners had limited ideas about what to do; their best notion was to use some of the golf course as a site for more public housing.

Cousins proposed a far different vision. Recognizing East Lake Golf Course's potential to become an economic engine for the renewal of the community, he purchased the course in 1993, razed the public housing project, and built a YMCA and a charter school. Then, in partnership with local faith-based and community leaders, Cousins built attractive, affordable housing, mixed in with market-rate homes. Today, East Lake Golf Course is once again playing host to PGA-tour competition, and its surrounding neighborhoods contain a vibrant mix of income levels.

Service Unites

St. Petersburg, Indianapolis, and Atlanta's redevelopment proves what can be done when government, business, and the nonprofit community work in partnership. President Bush's faith-based initiative and larger compassion agenda proves that government can be a catalyst for solving some of society's biggest human needs. Praxis, Venture Works, Billion + Change, and other efforts to mobilize treasure and talent for community well-being is a promising trend in the new millennium.

Each of these large endeavors requires the same formula: individuals willing to live for something greater than their own self-interest. They require advocates to say that desperate human needs are unacceptable when solutions exist. They require volunteers to trade comfort for consequential acts of service. And they require donors to exchange feel-good giving for results-focused social investments.

For those motivated by their Christian faith to serve, it is important to understand that the church is not a building or a "holy huddle." Instead, it is the people of God who are called to work together and with others to effectively and compassionately care for the world and its people that God loves so much.

For those motivated by their love of humanity or other goodwill, it is important to understand that helping people help themselves is superior to our intentions or the "helper's high" we receive by giving. We must define our success not only in how we serve others but in the ways we help renew their health and strength.

And regardless of motivation, it is important for all of us to pursue a service that unites. Social needs outpace the supply of effective solutions, requiring more volunteers, philanthropists, and social entrepreneurs to occupy their places on the frontlines. From the Minute Men who helped America win her independence to the neighborhood healers who renew it each day, our nation has relied on individual action rather than the state to advance its common good.

The tools of effective compassion best fit the hands of the individual. Godspeed in your efforts to serve your country by serving your communities.

APPENDIX A

A Brief History of How the White House Staff Evolved

When I gave tours to White House guests, I often pointed to a second-floor window of the residence where Abraham Lincoln delivered speeches to nineteenth-century visitors gathered on the north lawn. Spontaneously, crowds would sometimes form after large Civil War battles or other significant events, and Lincoln would eventually open the window and oblige them with commentary. My own guests' expressions would turn from wonder to disbelief when I explained that President Lincoln's entire operation was located in a couple rooms on that floor alongside the family's sleeping quarters. Indeed the famous Lincoln bedroom (as it is known today) was one of those offices.

These accommodations were surprisingly adequate given that President Lincoln only had a few paid White House assistants. That number was a few more than his earliest predecessors, such as the Adams and the Jeffersons, who were relegated to hiring family members out of their personal purse to serve as messengers and to complete other menial tasks. In contrast to John Adams, who penned his own correspondence, it is the duty of dozens of today's White House staffers to respond to the 60,000 letters sent to the president every week.

The Roosevelt cousins were the key change agents in creating the modern White House. It was Teddy Roosevelt who built the West Wing to accommodate a growing executive office staff that fit uncomfortably on the second floor of the residence along with his six children. There are conflicting accounts of whether the

West Wing was a product of Mrs. Roosevelt claiming that she was unable to run a family with all of the president's men around or Mr. Roosevelt claiming that he could not run a country with all his children running around. Likely a combination of both!

Nonetheless, the West Wing was built as America entered the Industrial Age and fought two world wars, adding much complexity to governing America's executive branch. The Brownlow Commission was formed to study the situation in 1933, and its report famously claimed, "The president needs help." In response, the commission recommended adding six assistants (described above as commissioned officers) who ideally would have "a passion for anonymity." Today's commissioned officers receive a parchment signed by the president and the secretary of state that reads, "Reposing special trust and confidence in your Integrity, Prudence and Ability, I do hereby appoint you..." Such language reminds each new occupant in those staff assistant positions of the history, virtue, and calling that comes with their service.

Presidential historian Bradley Patterson explains that by the end of World War II, the White House staff had grown to forty-five members and escalated to 400 under Eisenhower and 600 under Nixon. It was President Eisenhower, no doubt thanks to his military experience, who named the first chief of staff. Lyndon Johnson is the only successor to Eisenhower who managed White House affairs without the benefit of a chief. The White House staff structure continues to evolve, and in his latest book, Patterson cites the establishment of the faith-based office as one of the notable White House innovations as this institution entered its third century.[180]

---

[180] Bradley H. Patterson Jr., *To Serve the President: Continuity and Innovation in the White House Staff* (Washington, DC: Brookings Institution Press, 2008).

APPENDIX B

The following chart depicts a representative sample of the White House roundtables organized by each of the federal agency faith-based offices.

The President's Cabinet and the Compassion Agenda

Cabinet Agency Compassion in Action Roundtables United States Agency for International Development	– Social Enterprise in Africa – Combating Malaria – President's Emergency Plan for AIDS Relief (with State Department)
Corporation for National and Community Service	– National Service Strategies
Department of Agriculture	– Hunger
Commerce Department	– Inner-city Economic Development – Financial Literacy (with Treasury Department)
Education Department	– School Dropouts – Inner-city Private Schools
Health and Human Services	– Drug Treatment (with Drug Czar) – Mentoring – Healthy Families
Homeland Security	– Disaster Preparedness – Immigration Assimilation

Housing and Urban Development	– Homelessness
Justice Department	– Youth Violence – Human Trafficking (co-host with State Department)
Labor Department	– Prisoner Reentry

Full video of each session and companion materials are made available by Baylor University's Institute for Studies of Religion website (http://www.baylorisr.org/), and the Obama faith-based office features the federal agency centers' ongoing work on its blog (http://www.whitehouse.gov/administration/eop/ofbnp).

APPENDIX C

Eight Weeks in the Life of the White House Faith-Based Director

October 11—Keynote remarks to the Puerto Rico Governor's faith-based conference

October 23—Remarks to USAID worldwide mission director conference

October 24—Remarks to Compassion in Action Roundtable on Human Trafficking

October 25—Remarks to Compassion in Action Roundtable on Domestic Violence held at Baylor University

October 29—Remarks at National Constitutional Center event on faith-based initiatives with former director John DiIulio held at the University of Pennsylvania

November 1—Remarks at Mentoring Children of Prisoners event with First Lady Laura Bush in New Orleans, Louisiana

November 5—Remarks to White House faith-based conference in Indiana with Governor Mitch Daniels and Indianapolis Colts Head Coach Tony Dungy

November 7—Remarks to Compassion in Action Roundtable on Corporate Citizenship co-hosted by the U.S. Chamber of Commerce

November 8—Remarks at Helping America's Youth conference with First Lady Laura Bush in Dallas, Texas

November 11—Remarks at faith and foreign policy event at St. Anselm College in Manchester, New Hampshire

November 13—participate in America's Promise 10th anniversary dinner at White House State Dining Room

November 14—Remarks to International Social Justice conference at Heritage Foundation

November 16—Remarks at U.S. Department of Commerce urban economic development event with Kirbyjon Caldwell in Houston, Texas

November 27—Remarks at inaugural National Prisoner Re-entry Conference with Labor Secretary Elaine Chao in Los Angeles, California

November 28—Remarks to Saddleback Church AIDS conference with Pastor Rick Warren in Lake Forest, California

December 6—Policy Time with President Bush in Oval Office

December 12—Remarks to Compassion in Action Roundtable on World AIDS Day with Karen Hughes and Rick Warren

December 14—Remarks to Office Depot Foundation nonprofit conference in Boca Raton, Florida

During this same eight-week period, the twelve cabinet faith-based centers conducted training sessions for faith-based and community groups in Durham, North Carolina; Denver, Colorado; Minneapolis, Minnesota; Atlanta, Georgia; Indianapolis, Indiana; Montgomery, Alabama; Detroit, Michigan; Portland, Oregon; Tacoma, Washington; Jackson, Mississippi; and Dallas, Texas.

APPENDIX D

A Level Playing Field and New Partners

"The paramount goal is compassionate results, and private and charitable groups, including religious ones, should have the fullest opportunity permitted by law to compete on a level playing field, so long as they achieve valid public purposes.... The delivery of social services must be results-oriented and should value the bedrock principles of pluralism, nondiscrimination, evenhandedness, and neutrality."
—President George W. Bush January 29, 2001

President Bush calls for Charitable Choice to be made permanent. In his 2008 State of the Union address, President Bush called on Congress to permanently extend the Charitable Choice laws that currently ensure equal treatment of faith-based organizations in certain federal programs.

- Charitable Choice complies with legal standards established by the courts and protects the religious character of faith-based organizations participating in federally funded human service programs, while fully protecting the religious liberty of every individual seeking services from those programs. Charitable Choice principles have been adopted across the federal government through Equal Treatment rules adopted by federal agencies that host Centers for Faith-Based and Community Initiatives.

Gains in leveling the playing field. In 2001, the White House
OFBCI published a report titled *Unlevel Playing Field* that revealed
the findings of an audit of five federal agencies. The report identified
fifteen barriers inhibiting government partnerships with both faith-
based and other grassroots nonprofits and served as the blueprint
for sweeping change:

- President Bush signed Executive Order 13279 ordering federal agencies that administer social service programs not to
  discriminate against faith-based organizations based on their
  religious characters. The order established a new standard
  that judges organizations by their ability to deliver results
  rather than by their motivation for service.
- Cabinet agencies adopted the principles of Executive Order
  13279 through sixteen FBCI-related regulations, applying
  them to virtually every human service program sponsored by
  the federal government.

Opening the door for grassroots nonprofits. The challenge of
making government more welcoming to grassroots nonprofits
required the elimination of many additional barriers, including ending preferences for incumbent grantees in grant competitions and
introducing new policies to make programs accessible to smaller,
neighborhood organizations. Such polices included:

- Agencies revised the application materials and practices to sim-
  plify the process and disseminate information more effectively.
- Agencies removed unnecessary grant requirements that
  unduly burden smaller organizations and provided improved technical assistance with compliance and report-
  ing requirements.

- Intermediary Model Programs—Grants are awarded to large, veteran nonprofits that, in turn, sub-grant funds to grassroots nonprofits in their networks and deliver training and technical assistance to the sub-grantees and other grassroots groups, to increase their capacity to serve their community even after the grant has ended.
- Mini-grants—Agencies offer grants in the range of $10,000 to $75,000 that require less paperwork than typical large government grants. These right-sized grants enabled much leverage in private dollars added and volunteers recruited.
- Vouchers—Empowering beneficiaries to choose the service provider that best meets their unique needs allows many small-but-effective organizations to provide government-funded services for the first time, expanding their work and government's network of partner providers.

Training and Guidance. Even though the federal government had contracted with faith-based charities for decades, President Bush's Faith Based and Community Initiative was the first concerted effort to train policymakers and practitioners on clear, constitutional principles for government partnerships with religious nonprofit organizations.

- The White House OFBCI produced the first-ever guidebook defining the First Amendment parameters governing federal partnerships with faith-based organizations. This material has been distributed in hard copy and via the Internet to tens of thousands of readers.
- The guidebook and ancillary materials produced by the White House and Cabinet agencies were delivered through

dozens of conferences and workshops in all fifty states. Approximately 100,000 nonprofit leaders and state and local officials benefited from this training.

- Federal agency FBCI Centers work with career program staff to provide training materials and guidance documents to ensure that program administrators and grantees understand and comply with the legal parameters for use of federal funds and provide quality services to all eligible beneficiaries.

What They're Saying. Constitutional scholar and George Washington University law professor Robert Tuttle offered this assessment during a briefing on First Amendment jurisprudence at the 2007 annual conference of the Roundtable on Religion and Social Welfare: "I think we have seen about the most dramatic administrative change that is possible for those inside the Beltway to conceive... the idea that you go from a government that was in form as well as practice quite hostile to many kinds of religious organizations participating in government funding programs to one that has now institutionalized an expectation—it's not always practiced, but an expectation of equal treatment. I mean, that's a remarkable change and that's a change that didn't happen because of Charitable Choice although the groundwork was there. It's happened because of the Faith-Based and Community Initiative."

APPENDIX E

KEY MODERN ESTABLISHMENT CLAUSE CASES

Hein v. Freedom From Religion Foundation, 551 U.S. 587 (2007): The U.S. Supreme Court denied a constitutional challenge to the White House's regional conferences to strengthen government's partnership with faith-based and community organizations in providing social services to individuals across the nation. The original suit brought by the Freedom From Religion Foundation (FFRF) alleged that the Bush Administration was promoting funding for faith-based groups, thereby violating the Establishment Clause of the Constitution. Such characterization confuses equal treatment with favoritism and fails to comply with Court's consistent rulings over the past two decades clarifying that the Establishment Clause requires neutrality toward religion, not a prohibition on involvement of faith-based organizations in federal programs merely because of their religious character.

According to George Washington Law Professor Ira C. Lupu, a close observer of the faith-based initiative, "[T]his lawsuit was destined to lose. This was a very weak lawsuit on its merits. The government had very good reasons to sponsor these conferences. They said, 'Look, we want to promote the inclusion of faith-based organizations that heretofore have been excluded from participation in various federal programs.' It can't be unconstitutional just to invite them to apply for some kind of federal grants. And there's nothing wrong with government officers showing up at these conferences and saying good things about the power of faith organizations to contribute to the social good (64 Transcript of Opening Remarks,

Plenary Session: Acts of Law, Roundtable on Religion and Social Policy, p. 5–6; December 5, 2007).

Since none of the plaintiffs could point to a specific injury that they encountered as a result of these conferences, questions were raised about whether the federal court system has jurisdiction even to consider the matter. This was the ultimate question brought before the Supreme Court in Hein v Freedom from Religion Foundation and the court ruled on the side of the president and his initiative. In general, taxpayers cannot sue the federal government alleging a particular expenditure of funds is illegal based solely on their status as a taxpayer. The court held that FFRF was not entitled to an exception to this well-established rule."

Zelman v. Simmons-Harris, 536 U.S. 639 (2002): The U.S. Supreme Court approved a state program providing vouchers for children in a distressed public school district to attend private schools, including religious schools, as well as neighboring public schools. The court held that "where a government aid program is neutral with respect to religion, and provides assistance directly to a broad class of beneficiaries who, in turn, direct government aid to religious schools wholly as a result of their own genuine and independent private choice," the program does not violate the Establishment Clause.

Mitchell v. Helms, 530 U.S. 793 (2000): The court upheld a state and locally administered program that loaned educational materials, including books, computers, software, and audio/visual equipment to schools in economically disadvantaged areas, including religious schools. The program required schools receiving the aid to limit their use of the materials to "secular, neutral, and non-ideoligical" uses. A majority of the Court rejected the strict separationist theory that some organizations are too religious to participate in federal aid programs. The plurality described the pervasively sectarian distinction as "offensive," stating that, "[I]t is well established, in numerous other contexts, that courts should refrain from trolling through a person's or institution's religious beliefs," which "is just what [the pervasively sectarian distinction] requires." In her concurrence, Justice O'Connor, joined by Justice Breyer, held that for there to be a constitutional violation there must be actual diversion to religious use; providing public aid that merely "has the capacity for, or presents the possibility of, such diversion" is not automatically unconstitutional, thus essentially abandoning the pervasively sectarian standard.

Agostini v. Felton, 521 US 203 (1997): In *Agostini*, the court took the rare step of explicitly overturning two of its strict separationist decisions. The court upheld a program providing remedial education to students of private schools (including religious schools), in which instruction is given on the premises of those schools by public employees. The court acknowledged that its Establishment Clause jurisprudence had significantly changed since the 1970s and '80s, especially with regard to its understanding of what constitutes an impermissible effect of state indoctrination of religion or constitutes a "symbolic union between government and religion." The court did not examine the character of the organizations aided by the program, and instead focused on whether any advancement of religion was reasonably attributable to the government.

Bowen v. Kendrick, 487 US 589 (1988): In *Bowen*, the court upheld the constitutionality of the Adolescent Family Life Act (AFLA), which authorizes federal grants to public and nonprofit organizations, including faith-based organizations, for services and research in the area of premarital adolescent sexual relations and pregnancy. The court rejected the notion that a program that is facially neutral between secular and religious applicants would necessarily advance religion in violation of the Establishment Clause, noting that the AFLA contained no requirement that grantees be affiliated with any religious denomination and that there was "nothing inherently religious" about the education and counseling activities funded by the program.

Witters v. Washington, 474 US 481 (1986): In *Witters*, the court approved a state program designed to provide vocational training to the blind under which beneficiaries could use state tuition grants at religiously affiliated colleges and to pursue ministerial degrees. The court held that because the grants were "made available generally without regard to the sectarian-nonsectarian, or public–private nature of the institution benefited," and flowed to religious organizations "only as a result of the genuinely independent and private choices of individuals," the program did not have the effect of advancing religion.

Source: *White House FBCI;* "The Quiet Revolution: The President's Faith-Based and Community Initiative: A Seven-Year Progress Report," The White House (2008).

APPENDIX F

THE WHITE HOUSE—QUIET
REVOLUTION—JUNE 2008

A LEVEL PLAYING FIELD AND NEW PARTNERS

The Faith-Based and Community Initiative is built on the premise that government will most effectively address human need when it draws upon the strength of every willing partner. Yet when President Bush took office in January 2001, it was clear that two types of groups were not always welcome to work in partnership with the government: nonprofits motivated to service by their faith, and grassroots organizations lacking grant-writing skills and insight into the federal grant process.

In response, the president required his federal agencies to eliminate every unwarranted barrier to government partnerships with any faith-based or grassroots nonprofit capable of effectively delivering services to the needy. This work commenced in the second week of George W. Bush's presidency. On January 29, 2001, President Bush signed Executive Orders 13198 and 13199 creating the White House Office of Faith-Based and Community Initiatives (OFBCI), five initial Centers for Faith-Based and Community Initiatives within federal agencies, and an agenda for the Initiative that ended discrimination against faith-based and grassroots nonprofit organizations.

Standing behind him during the signing ceremony were Catholic, Jewish, Protestant, and Muslim leaders as well as secular nonprofit leaders, foundation officials, and others. The president articulated his vision of America as a pluralistic nation including good citizens of different faiths or of no faith at all, united in concern for those who live in the shadows of a society suffering from addiction and violence, homelessness and hopelessness. The president acknowledged that Americans share a common calling to respond to such needs. He emphasized the rightful responsibilities of government, yet he said that when the toughest social problems arise, requiring love of one's neighbor as self, his administration would look first to faith-based programs and community groups. He pledged not to fund the religious activities of any group, but he also affirmed that government would not discriminate against effective nonprofits because of their faith.

The Executive Orders gave the FBCI its marching orders. For starters, Executive Order 13198 required the five federal agency-based centers to:

> Conduct, in coordination with the White House OFBCI, a department-wide audit to identify all existing barriers to the participation of faith-based and other community organizations in the delivery of social services by the department, including but not limited to regulations, rules, orders, procurement, and other internal policies and practices, and outreach activities that either facially discriminate against or otherwise discourage or disadvantage the participation of faith-based and other community organizations in federal programs.

The results of these audits were published in an August 2001 report titled "Unlevel Playing Field: Barriers to Participation by Faith-Based and Community Organizations in Federal Social Service Programs."

The report identified fifteen obstacles faced by faith-based and grassroots organizations that inhibited their ability to serve neighbors in need (see text box below). This appendix describes the nature of these obstacles, the reformations fostered by a team of Bush Administration officials and dedicated career civil servants at eleven federal agencies, and the guidance and training offered to government officials and nonprofit leaders to avoid bureaucratic mistakes and legal misinterpretations in the future.

Obstacles initially faced by faith-based organizations seeking to partner with government:

- A pervasive suspicion of faith-based organizations on the part of many government officials
- The total exclusion of faith-based organizations from some federal programs
- Excessive restrictions on religious activities
- Inappropriate expansion of restrictions on religious activities to new programs
- The denial of faith-based organizations' legally established right to take religion into account in employment decisions
- Failure to require and assist state and local officials in complying with Charitable Choice

Obstacles initially faced by small nonprofits, faith-based and secular, seeking to partner with government:

- Limited accessibility of federal grant information
- Heavy burden of regulations and other requirements
- Heavy requirements that have to be met before a group can apply for funds

- Complex grant applications and grant agreements
- Questionable favoritism in some programs toward faith-based organizations
- Improper bias in some programs in favor of previous grantees
- Inappropriate requirement to apply in collaboration with likely competitors
- Requiring 501(c)(3) status where a program statute requires only nonprofit status
- Inadequate attention in the federal grant streamlining process to faith-based and community organizations

Source: *"Unlevel Playing Field: Barriers to Participation by Faith-Based and Community Organizations in Federal Social Service Programs"* The White House (August 2001).

Seven years after the FBCI's inception, the federal government has become far more welcoming to the faith-based and community partnerships that the president envisioned. Foundational to this achievement are sixteen rule changes affecting virtually all human-service programs across government. These regulatory changes have been complemented by concerted action by federal agencies to eliminate barriers to participation by grassroots nonprofits, both secular and faith-based, and the development of innovative program models for expanding partnerships with small and novice grassroots organizations. It is difficult to overstate the significance of leveling what was once a tilted playing field that disfavored possibly the most helpful and engaged organizations in solving the greatest social challenges facing the nation. Constitutional scholar and George Washington University law professor Robert Tuttle put it this way:

> I think we have seen about the most dramatic administrative change that is possible for those inside the Beltway to conceive ... the idea that you go from a government that was

in form as well as practice quite hostile to many kinds of religious organizations participating in government funding programs to one that has now institutionalized an expectation—it's not always practiced, but an expectation of equal treatment. I mean, that's a remarkable change and that's a change that didn't happen because of Charitable Choice although the groundwork was there. It's happened because of the Faith-Based and Community Initiative.[181]

To comprehend the magnitude of this accomplishment, it is necessary to understand the federal government's shift from adherence to and application of the Supreme Court's pervasively sectarian standard to the equal treatment standards adopted by the court over the past couple decades. While the federal courts began moving in this direction in the 1980s, the federal government did not follow suit until President Bush's executive orders required it to do so.

Movement toward Neutrality in First Amendment Jurisprudence

Prior to the mid-twentieth century, the U.S. Supreme Court considered very few cases involving the Establishment Clause of the First Amendment. By the 1970s, the court had interpreted the clause to prohibit government aid to religious organizations deemed to be "pervasively sectarian," meaning that groups with strong religious orientation were prohibited from participating in otherwise widely available public programs. The court's early cases nearly all dealt with the government providing direct financial assistance (cash or

---

[181] Lew Daly, *God's Economy: Faith-Based Initiatives & the Caring State* (Chicago: University of Chicago Press, 2009): 65.

in kind) to religious schools.[182] This pervasively sectarian doctrine required the courts to examine the religious beliefs and practices of religious organizations on a case-by-case basis to determine whether a "substantial portion of its functions are subsumed in [its] religious mission...."[183]

In the 1980s, the court began moving away from a strict separationist paradigm to a philosophy of neutrality, one that promotes pluralism and nondiscrimination and refrains from using the power of the government purse to coerce individuals' or organizations' religious beliefs or practices. A neutral policy provides equal access to government-sponsored programs and forums without requiring forfeiture of religious speech or character. Under the neutrality paradigm, the constitutionality of financial assistance provided directly to an organization rests on the type and

---

[182] See *Aguilar v. Felton*, 473 US 402 (1985) (invalidating remedial education for disadvantaged students that was delivered by public school teachers on campuses of religious schools); *Grand Rapids Sch. Dist. v. Ball*, 473 US 373 (1985) (invalidating supplemental courses taught by public school teachers on campuses of religious schools); *Wolman v. Walter*, 433 US 229 (1977) (invalidating state program to provide instructional materials to religious schools); *Roemer v. Maryland Pub. Works Bd.*, 426 US 736 (1976) (permitting state program providing non-categorical grants to religiously affiliated colleges, provided the colleges are not pervasively sectarian and the grants are not used for sectarian purposes); *Meek v. Pettinger*, 421 US 349 (1975) (invalidating state program to provide instructional materials to religious schools); *Hunt v. McNair*, 413 US 734, 743 (1973) (permitting state program to provide bonds for construction of buildings at religiously affiliated colleges, provided college not pervasively sectarian and buildings not used for sectarian purposes); *Levitt v. Committee for Pub. Ed.*, 413 US 472 (1973) (invalidating state payments for state-required tests designed and graded by teachers in religious schools); *Lemon v. Kurtzman*, 403 US 602, (1971) (invalidating state payments for portion of salaries of teachers in religious schools, textbooks, and instructional materials); *Tilton v. Richardson*, 403 US 672 (1971) (permitting federal program to provide grants for construction of buildings at religiously affiliated colleges, provided college not pervasively sectarian and buildings not used for sectarian purposes). See also Ira C. Lupu and Robert W. Tuttle, *Government Partnerships with Faith-Based Providers: State of the Law* (2002); Ira C. Lupu, testimony before the Committee on the Judiciary, Subcommittee on the Constitution, US House of Representatives, June 7, 2001; Douglas Laycock, *The Underlying Unity of Separation and Neutrality*, 46 Emory L. J. 43 (1997).

[183] *Hunt*, 413 US 734, 743 (1973).

use of such aid, instead of focusing on the nature or beliefs of the organization.[184]

In its modern neutrality precedents, the Supreme Court made clear that faith-based organizations may participate as grantees of federal social-service programs, provided there is "nothing inherently religious" about services provided under the program.[185] Indeed, the court added that Congress may "recognize[e] the important part that religion or religious organizations may play in resolving certain secular problems."[186] The court abandoned the "pervasively sectarian" standard, permitting religious organizations to participate in neutral, secular direct-aid programs, provided the aid is limited to secular uses and not diverted to religious uses.[187] The constitutionality of a federal program rests on the use of the aid provided, rather than the character of the organization receiving the aid.

The Supreme Court has also set forth distinct guidelines for programs that allow participants real choice among multiple service providers. Such programs do not provide government funds directly to organizations, but rather to individual participants, so the funding approach is referred to as "indirect aid." In choice-based programs

---

[184] See Ira C. Lupu and Robert W. Tuttle, *Government Partnerships with Faith-Based Providers: State of the Law* (2002); Ira C. Lupu, testimony before the Committee on the Judiciary, Subcommittee on the Constitution, US House of Representatives, June 7, 2001; Eric W. Treene, *Religion, the Public Square, and the Presidency*, 24 Harv. J.L. and Pub. Pol'y 573 (2001); Carl H. Esbeck, *Myths, Miscues, and Misconceptions: No-Aid Separationism and the Establishment Clause*, 13 Notre Dame J.L. Ethics and Pub. Pol'y 285 (1999); Douglas Laycock, *The Underlying Unity of Separation and Neutrality*, 46 Emory L.J. 43 (1997); Stephen V. Monsma and J. Christopher Sopher, eds., *Equal Treatment of Religion in a Pluralistic Society* (1998).

[185] See *Mitchell v. Helms*, 530 US 793 (2000) (permitting state-administered program loaning secular educational materials and equipment to public and private schools, including religious schools); *Agostini v. Felton*, 521 US 203 (1997) (permitting remedial education for disadvantaged students that was delivered by public school teachers on campuses of religious schools); *Bowen v. Kendrick*, 487 US 589 (1988) (upholding participation of religious organizations in adolescent pregnancy education and services grant program).

[186] *Bowen*, 487 US at 607.

[187] *Mitchell*, 530 US 793, 853-60 (O'Connor, J., concurring in the judgment)

that deliver services using "indirect aid," the Supreme Court shifted its focus from the nature of the organization providing the services to the nature of the choice provided to the individual beneficiary.[188] The court held that "where a government-aid program is neutral with respect to religion, and provides assistance directly to a broad class of beneficiaries who, in turn, direct government aid to religious [organizations] wholly as a result of their own genuine and independent private choice," the program is constitutional.[189] In such programs, faith-based organizations are not required to alter their religious identity or separate religious activities, as any religious indoctrination that may take place is the result of the choice of the individual, rather than the government.[190]

Restrictive Federal Policy

The 2001 audits of social service programs at the Departments of Health and Human Services (HHS), Housing and Urban Development (HUD), Education, Justice (DOJ), and Labor (DOL) found that some federal agencies retained both formal and informal barriers to funding "pervasively sectarian" organizations despite the U.S. Supreme Court's repudiation of the doctrine. Specific examples

---

[188] See *Zelman v. Simmons-Harris*, 536 US 639 (2002) (upholding a state program permitting parents to use vouchers at religiously affiliated schools); *Zobrest v. Catalinia Foothills Sch. Dist.*, 509 U.S. 1 (1993) (permitting a student to receive state-funded sign language interpretation services at a religiously affiliated school); *Witters v. Washington*, 474 US 481 (1986) (upholding a program permitting tuition grants to be used at religiously affiliated colleges and for ministerial studies); *Mueller v. Allen*, 463 US 388 (1983) (upholding a state tax deduction for private school tuition paid to religiously affiliated schools).

[189] *Zelman*, 536 US at 652.

[190] See *Zelman v. Simmons-Harris*, 536 US 639 (2002) (upholding a state program permitting parents to use vouchers at religiously affiliated schools); *Zobrest v. Catalinia Foothills Sch. Dist.*, 509 US 1 (1993) (permitting a student to receive state-funded sign language interpretation services at a religiously affiliated school); *Witters v. Washington*, 474 US 481 (1986) (upholding a program permitting tuition grants to be used at religiously affiliated colleges and for ministerial studies); *Mueller v. Allen*, 463 US 388 (1983) (upholding a state tax deduction for private school tuition paid to religiously affiliated schools).

of "a widespread bias against faith-based and community organizations in federal social service programs" included:

1) Restricting some kinds of religious organizations from applying for funding
2) Restricting religious activities that are not prohibited by the Constitution
3) Not honoring rights that religious organizations have under federal law
4) Burdening small organizations with cumbersome regulations and requirements
5) Imposing anti-competitive mandates on some programs, such as requiring applicants to demonstrate support from government agencies or others that might also be competing for the same funds[191]

While some limitations on religious organizations within a federal program are constitutionally required and appropriate, the audit found that many federal policies and practices went well beyond constitutional and legislative requirements, arising from an overriding misperception by federal officials "that close collaboration with religious organizations was legally suspect."[192] These policies and practices included:

- Bans or other limitations on some or all religious organizations applying for funding
- Requiring applicants to alter or disguise their religious character to be eligible for funding

---

[191] *Unlevel Playing Field: Barriers to Participation by Faith-Based and Community Organizations in Federal Social Service Programs*, p. 2 (2001).

[192] *Unlevel Playing Field: Barriers to Participation by Faith-Based and Community Organizations in Federal Social Service Programs*, p. 10 (2001).

- Requiring religious organizations to forfeit their right under Title VII of the Civil Rights Act of 1964 to staff on a religious basis
- Providing lists of prohibited religious activities without a positive affirmation of eligibility or guidance on how faith-based organizations can legally and effectively partner with government
- Excessive restrictions on constitutionally permissible religious activities

For example, the U.S. Department of Housing and Urban Development's regulations for the Community Development Block Grant (CDBG) program (which provides federal funds to localities to support nongovernmental services) and for the HOME program (which gives funds to states and localities who often enlist community groups in efforts to provide affordable housing) prohibited funding "as a general rule" from going to "primarily religious" organizations for "any activities, including secular activities." Under the HOME program, a "primarily religious" organization could establish a "wholly secular entity" that could then take part in the program. In the CDBG program, a further regulation provided that a "primarily religious" organization could take part if it agreed to a long list of restrictions, which included forfeiting its Title VII rights (a restriction not required by the authorizing statute). Similarly, the Department of Education's guidance for the Even Start Family Literacy Program prohibited "pervasively sectarian" organizations from receiving direct funds under the program and permitted such organizations to participate only as a subordinate to a "nonsectarian" partner organization. Even where a program's regulations or guidance documents did not specifically invoke the pervasively sectarian distinction, the audit found some federal, state, and local program staff applied a similar, unwritten standard resulting in the exclusion of some faith-based organizations.[193]

Additionally, where faith-based organizations were permitted to participate, some federal agencies and their state or local administrators placed excessive restrictions on religious activities that were not required by constitutional law. For example, Head Start programs, often located in houses of worship, were sometimes locally pressured to remove or cover up religious art, symbols, or other items.[194] Other faith-based organizations applying for locally administrated programs were told they would be ineligible unless they removed references to "God" from their mission statements or removed religious symbols from their walls.[195]

Workforce Investment Act Job Training Vouchers

Under the Workforce Investment Act (WIA), the U.S. Department of Labor (DOL) provides a voucher-like system where an individual beneficiary selects from a range of qualified job training programs and providers. The program requires the beneficiary, rather than the federal government, to choose the course of study and the provider; however, regulations prohibited beneficiaries from using indirect federal funds "to be employed or trained in sectarian activities." This federal policy stood in clear contrast to guidance from the U.S. Supreme Court, which for over twenty years had made clear that, when a program or provider is chosen by a private citizen and not designated by government, prohibiting training in

---

[193] *Unlevel Playing Field: Barriers to Participation by Faith-Based and Community Organizations in Federal Social Service Programs*, p.11 (2001).

[194] *Unlevel Playing Field: Barriers to Participation by Faith-Based and Community Organizations in Federal Social Service Programs* p.14 (2001).

[195] *Unlevel Playing Field: Barriers to Participation by Faith-Based and Community Organizations in Federal Social Service Programs* p.14 (2001).

religious vocations is not required by the Establishment Clause.[196] With assistance from its Center for Faith-Based and Community Initiatives, DOL revised its rules governing the WIA to allow for more choice and greater freedom by permitting beneficiaries of voucher-style programs to use that indirect funding to train for religious vocations.[197]

Charitable Choice as the First Step to Equal Treatment

While First Amendment case law replaced the pervasively sectarian standard with equal treatment principles over the past two decades, no parallel transition was occurring in policy-making at the federal agencies until the mid-1990s when Congress acted several times, by bipartisan majorities, to reduce barriers to participation by faith-based organizations in federal social service delivery and to respond to the Supreme Court's more neutral, pluralistic interpretations of the Establishment Clause. Congress' remedy to the barriers faith-based organizations faced in several major federal social service programs comprised a set of federal laws known as "Charitable Choice."

Charitable Choice was first enacted in the 1996 Personal Responsibility and Work Opportunities Reform Act[198] and covered state and local spending of Temporary Assistance to Needy Families (TANF) funds used to obtain services. Charitable Choice language was added to several additional programs, including the Welfare-to-Work program in 1997; the Community Services Block Grant (CSBG)

---

[196] See *Zelman v. Simmons-Harris*, 536 US 639 (2002) (upholding a state program permitting parents to use vouchers at religiously affiliated schools); *Zobrest v. Catalinia* Foothills Sch. Dist., 509 US 1 (1993) (permitting a student to receive state-funded sign language interpretation services at a religiously affiliated school); *Witters v. Washington*, 474 US 481 (1986) (upholding a program permitting tuition grants to be used at religiously affiliated colleges and for ministerial studies); *Mueller v. Allen*, 463 US 388 (1983) (upholding a state tax deduction for private school tuition paid to religiously affiliated schools).

[197] 20 C.F.R. Part 667.266(b)(1).

[198] 42 U.S.C. Sec. 604a.

program in 1998; and the Substance Abuse Prevention and Treatment Block Grant, the Projects for Assistance in Transition from Homelessness formula program, and the discretionary substance abuse treatment programs administered by the Substance Abuse and Mental Health Services Administration (SAMHSA) in 2000.

Charitable Choice provisions required program administrators to permit faith-based providers to compete in covered programs without abandoning their religious character or mission, while protecting the religious liberty of individual beneficiaries and prohibiting the use of direct federal funds for inherently religious activities. Unfortunately, although the language of the statutes enacting Charitable Choice made its provisions mandatory for the covered programs, the 2001 audit of federal social-service programs found that the provisions "had been almost entirely ignored by federal administrators, who had done little to help or require state and local governments to comply with the new rules for participation by faith-based providers."[199] Specifically, the Charitable Choice provisions had been insufficiently incorporated into the agencies' grant-making rules and procedures, and state and local governments had received almost no guidance as to how to comply with the new rules for participation by faith-based providers.

In 2002, HHS, which administers the TANF, CSBG, and SAMHSA substance abuse treatment programs, announced regulations to fully implement the Charitable Choice provisions and to provide guidance to State and local administrators, as well as to faith-based organizations, regarding the provisions' practical application.[200]

---

[199] *Unlevel Playing Field: Barriers to Participation by Faith-Based and Community Organizations in Federal Social Service Programs* p.2 (2001).

[200] 45 C.F.R. Part 260 (implementing Charitable Choice provisions of TANF); 45 C.F.R. Part 1050 (implementing Charitable Choice provisions of CSBG); 42 CFR Parts 54, 54a, and 96 (implementing Charitable Choice provisions of SAMHSA).

The core principles of Charitable Choice regulations are reflected in the equal treatment principles set out in Executive Order 13279 and in the agencies' equal treatment regulations (discussed below). However, some principles are applied in slightly different ways to their respective programs, and some additional provisions are unique to certain Charitable Choice statutes.[201]

Fulfilling Charitable Choice Principles through Executive Orders

Charitable Choice provisions provided solid legal guidelines for how government could adopt the Supreme Court's modern neutrality principles in partnerships with faith-based organizations. However, these provisions governed only five major programs. Even more significantly, as noted above, they had been widely ignored by the federal, state, and local officials charged with putting them into action. Executive Order 13279 changed this by applying Charitable Choice principles to virtually all federal programs serving the needy *and* by requiring robust action to ensure they were fully applied. Executive Order 13279 provides that "[n]o organization should be discriminated against on the basis of religion or religious belief in the administration or distribution of federal financial assistance under social-service programs."

This provision directs federal agencies to end discrimination against organizations based on their religious character, and prohibits government from favoring organizations of one faith over another or from preferring religious organizations to secular ones. It

---

[201] Provisions in SAMHSA and TANF laws, for example, require implementing agencies to allow beneficiaries to receive services from an alternate provider if the beneficiary objects to receiving services from a religious provider. Statutory provisions for CSBG and SAMHSA require faith-based organizations to maintain separate accounts for the federal funds they receive. See 45 C.F.R. Part 260 (implementing Charitable Choice provisions of TANF); 45 C.F.R. Part 1050 (implementing Charitable Choice provisions of CSBG); 42 CFR Parts 54, 54a, and 96 (implementing Charitable Choice provisions of SAMHSA).

focuses government less on the organization's mission statement or beliefs and more on the organization's ability to effectively deliver services. Executive Order 13279 also provides clear, uniform guidance on the constitutionally required restrictions on the use of federal funds. In accordance with the Establishment Clause and the Free Exercise Clause, "...organizations that engage in inherently religious activities, such as worship, religious instruction, and proselytization, must offer those services separately in time or location from any programs or services supported with direct federal financial assistance, and participation in any such inherently religious activities must be voluntary for the beneficiaries of the social service program supported with such federal financial assistance."[202] The Executive Order 13279 also protects freedom of religion by directing the agencies administering social service programs to prohibit organizations receiving financial assistance from discriminating against eligible beneficiaries of those social services programs "on the basis of religion, a religious belief, a refusal to hold a religious belief, or a refusal to actively participate in a religious practice."[203]

Introduction of the Equal Treatment Regulations Implementing the Executive Orders through Agency Rule Changes

Upon publication of the President's Executive Order 13279 requiring "Equal Protection of the Laws for Faith-Based and Community Organizations" and with additional guidance from the U.S. Department of Justice (DOJ), federal agencies considered how to appropriately and constitutionally implement the FBCI. Federal social-service programs vary greatly in size, content, and structure,

---

[202] Exec. Order No. 13279 (December 12, 2002).
[203] Exec. Order No. 13279 (December 12, 2002).

and each agency that administers federal social-service programs has separate regulations, policies, and procedures, even among their own component organizations. Rules and practices may even vary from program to program. Therefore, regulatory and other administrative reforms needed to be tailored to individual agencies and programs. Nine federal agencies have produced fifteen final rules, including general rules that cover the programs administered by seven agencies,[204] three regulations implementing the Charitable Choice statutes,[205] a U.S. Department of Labor (DOL) regulation permitting faith-based contractors to retain their Title VII right to take faith into account in making employment decisions,[206] and four regulations changing discriminatory or unnecessarily limiting language in specific HUD, Veterans Affairs, Commerce, and DOL programs.[207] A proposed sixteenth rule covering programs administered by the Department of Homeland Security was published on January 14, 2008.[208] The general rules for programs administered by HUD, USDA, HHS, USAID, Education, DOJ, DOL, and DHS closely follow the principles and guidance provided by Executive Order 13279. Each provides an affirmation that faith-based organizations are eligible to participate in federal

[204] 28 CFR Parts 31, 33, 38, 90, 91, and 93 (Justice); 34 CFR Parts 74, 75, 76, 80 (Education); 24 CFR Parts 5 and 570 (HUD general programs); 24 CFR Parts 954 and 1003 (HUD Indian programs); 7 CFR Part 16 (USDA); 45 CFR Parts 74, 92, 96, and 87 (HHS); 20 CFR Parts 667, 670 and 29 CFR 2, 37 (Labor); 22 CFR Parts 202, 205, 211, and 226 (USAID).

[205] 45 C.F.R. Part 260 (implementing Charitable Choice provisions of TANF); 45 C.F.R. Part 1050 (implementing Charitable Choice provisions of CSBG); 42 CFR Parts 54, 54a, and 96 (implementing Charitable Choice provisions of SAMHSA).

[206] 41 C.F.R. Part 60-1.5.

[207] 24 CFR Parts 92, 570, 572, 574, 576, 582, 583, and 585 (amending regulations for eight HUD programs); 38 CFR Part 61 (amending VA Homelessness Providers Grant and Per Diem programs); 20 CFR Parts 667, 670 and 29 CFR 2, 37, 29 CFR Part 37 (amending regulations for Labor's WIA and Job Corps); 13 CFR Chapter III (Commerce's Economic Development Administration programs).

[208] 73 F.R. 2187.

social-service programs on the same basis as any other private organization and that entities distributing federal funds cannot discriminate either for or against an organization on the basis of religion or religious belief.

These rules also ensure that these programs are implemented in a manner consistent with the Supreme Court's interpretation of the Constitution. The regulations make clear that direct federal funds cannot be used to support inherently religious activities, such as worship, religious instruction, and proselytizing. If an organization conducts such activities, the activities must be offered separately, in time or location, from the programs or services funded with direct federal financial assistance, and participation must be voluntary for beneficiaries of the programs or services funded with such assistance. The rules also reflect the different standard enunciated by the Supreme Court for programs of indirect aid, which permit inherently religious activities to be part of a funded program where the program is selected via a genuine and independent private choice of a beneficiary, provided the religious organizations otherwise satisfy the requirements of the program. The general regulations promulgated provide clear and detailed guidance regarding faith-based organizations' religious character, independence, and religious activities, very closely tracking the language of Executive Order 13279. They also confirm the Title VII right of faith-based organizations to select employees who share their vision and mission, including religious beliefs, under all of the grant programs covered by the regulations.

The notable exception to this protection of Title VII hiring rights are grant programs governed by authorizing statutes that prohibit all grantees from considering religious beliefs in employment decisions. In such programs, applicants are directed to consult with the relevant program office to determine the scope of these requirements. As discussed below, in some cases other independent statutory provisions may supersede this prohibition, particularly the Religious Freedom Restoration Act (RFRA).

Prior to the issuance of Executive Order 13279 and subsequent regulatory changes, no federal government-wide standard prohibited religious discrimination by directly financed providers against eligible beneficiaries of the funded services. With regard to the rights of individuals served by federal social-service programs, the general regulations following from Executive Order 13279 make clear that organizations may not discriminate against any eligible "program beneficiary or prospective program beneficiary on the basis of religion or religious belief."[209]

The general regulations also contain provisions prohibiting federal program officers or state or local administrators from disqualifying religious organizations because of their religious motivation, character, or affiliation or from requiring only faith-based organizations to sign assurances that they will not use direct funds for inherently religious activities. They provide guidance to state and local administrators regarding the legal effect of commingling federal funds, and they clarify that nonprofit organizations, religious or secular, are not required to obtain federal 501(c)(3) status in order to be eligible for funding (unless specifically required by a particular program's authorizing statute).[210]

---

[209] 28 C.F.R. Part 38.1(d).

[210] Nonprofits which have not applied for 501(c)(3) status may demonstrate their nonprofit status via a statement from a state taxing body or the state secretary of state certifying that the organization is a nonprofit organization operating within the State and that no part of its net earnings may lawfully benefit any private shareholder or individual, or a certified copy of the applicant's certificate of incorporation or similar document that clearly establishes the nonprofit status of the organization. Chapters of a larger state or national nonprofit organization may demonstrate their status with copy of any qualifying document issued to the parent organization, together with a statement by the State or parent organization that the applicant is a local nonprofit affiliate.

ACKNOWLEDGMENTS

First, my appreciation goes to President and Mrs. Bush. It was President Bush's vision to rally America's armies of compassion and to invent the faith-based initiative as catalyst for his determined attack on need. Both he and Mrs. Bush led with vigor, inspiration, and grace.

When my family first arrived in Washington, I took them to watch the Bushes land on the White House lawn in Marine One following their Thanksgiving weekend at Camp David. We didn't expect to visit with the president, but he took the time to greet my wife, Mary Jo, and then shook hands with my sons, T.J. and Ryan. Making direct eye contact with each of the boys, he said, "I want to thank you for the sacrifice you made so that your dad can work for me. You left your school and your friends back home. I know that is a hard thing to do, and I'm grateful."

That is George Bush. The son of a politician, he knows how hard it is for the families who support men and women in public life. As a father of daughters, he knows how much it means to invest in children. And as a boss loyal to his team, his investments in staff modeled how we should likewise invest in our teams as well as other Americans visiting the White House.

My gratefulness for noble leadership at the top was matched by the joy of working alongside the best young talent in the compassionate conservative movement. Those who came to Washington to serve in the faith-based offices were drawn by mission not title. They were idealistic, creative, and highly skilled.

There were hundreds of faith-based staff who preceded me and served under the able leadership of my colleagues John Dilulio and Jim Towey. You all served with distinction and set a foundation for a new generation of government partnerships with the social sector.

To those who served in the federal agencies during my time in the White House, thank you for joining me in the effort to build on our predecessors' success, growing the initiative across the states, and pointing it toward the nation's sorest human needs.

To my staff in the White House, I'll forever be in your debt. You became my partners in one of the grandest adventures in government: to reform government and revitalize society at the same time. Thank you for helping me *serve the servants* and for making those living in the shadows of society the true object of our endeavors.

I have created a webpage at Baylor University's "Faith in Action" website dedicated to all of President Bush's faith-based initiative staff. Please visit the page and share your stories about how you are furthering the cause that united us in the Bush administration.

This book is one expression of my post–White House service, and it was made possible by the generosity of two institutions whose leaders have supplied much thought leadership to the faith-based movement. First, I want to thank Baylor University for welcoming me as a fellow and charging me with this book assignment.

My dear friend Byron Johnson directs the Institute for Studies of Religion at Baylor, and he has stood among the world's foremost scholars of the "faith factor." It was his encouragement more than anyone else that spurred my thinking and writing on the themes of this book. And it is my great privilege to work them out day by day as his colleague.

Next, I want to thank the Lynde and Harry Bradley Foundation for supplying a research grant for me to begin work on this book and for its longstanding support of civil society thought leadership. In particular, my gratitude is owed to Dan Schmidt and

Mike Hartmann, who have been my partners in this and other similar endeavors.

It is one thing to write a book and quite another altogether to publish it. The events that transpired to move my draft chapters into a finished product are simply providential. Cliff Johnson of Christianity Today taught me the business and led me with great expertise. His colleague, Jim Bolton, brought a creative eye and careful attention to detail.

The fact that Christianity Today served as the book's business agent is a poetic echo of its earlier stimulus for me to live my faith in the public policy mission field. It was a 1985 article in *International Christianity Today* by Chuck Colson that introduced me to the life example of William Wilberforce. From the moment I read that article, I have hungered to seek justice in policy and enhance service through private charities.

It is a happy coincidence that my book was ready for market at the same time Tammy Faxel was launching an important new venture at Amazon. Her extensive publishing experience led Amazon to recruit her to build a new imprint for faith-based readers, and she paid me the high and undeserved honor of being one of her first authors. Her company's initiative represents an important new chapter in Christian publishing, and I'm delighted to be a part of it.

Of course, my deepest gratitude goes to my family who supported my writing and more so my work during our shared season in the White House. God has blessed us richly and it is my life's sweetest ambition to love Mary Jo, Ali, T.J., and Ryan as I have been loved.

To those who love neighbor as self, this book is written in hopes that your stories will be better understood and that your efforts will receive more appreciation and support. To God who is love, thank you for blessing us to be a blessing to others.

ABOUT THE AUTHOR

 Jay F. Hein is president of Sagamore Institute, an Indianapolis-based think tank he co-founded with U.S. Senator Dan Coats in 2004. He was Deputy Assistant to the President and Director of the White House Office of Faith-Based and Community Initiatives from 2006 to 2008. Hein serves as Distinguished Senior Fellow at Baylor University's Institute for the Study of Religion and he directs the ISOKO Institute, an African think tank aimed at enterprise solutions to poverty.

Earlier in his career, Hein was a welfare reform policy advisor to Governor Tommy Thompson of Wisconsin and director of civil society programs at the Hudson Institute. Hein received a Bachelors of Arts degree from Eureka College and an Honorary Doctor of Laws from Indiana Wesleyan University where he is developing the Ron Blue Institute.

Hein is author of *Quiet Revolution – Transforming the World through Faith and Service;* co-author of *The New Wisconsin Idea – Reinventing Public Compassion for the 21st Century;* and Editor-in-Chief of American Outlook, a quarterly public policy journal.